DREADNOUGHTS AND SUPER-DREADNOUGHTS

CASEMATE | ILLUSTRATED | SPECIAL

C CASEMATE | ILLUSTRATED | SPECIAL

DREADNOUGHTS AND SUPER-DREADNOUGHTS

CHRIS McNAB

Photo credits: The images in this work are taken from both the author's own collection and a range of public domain, copyright-free, and Creative Commons sources, including Nick-D, Nick Dowling, Tony Hisgett, George Grantham Bain Collection, Daniel Schwen, Adam Cuerden, Library of Congress, National Archives and Records Administration (NARA), U.S. Navy, Shutterstock (Everett Collection/Shutterstock.com), National Museum of the U.S. Navy, Serviço de Divulgação da Marinha do Brasil, State Library of Victoria, Science Museum Group, Kure Maritime Museum, Jef Maytom, and Nigel Aspdin. Thanks also go to the National Maritime Museum.

CISS0009

Published in the United States of America and Great Britain in 2021 by

CASEMATE PUBLISHERS
1950 Lawrence Road, Havertown, PA 19083, USA
and
The Old Music Hall, 106–108 Cowley Road, Oxford OX4 1JE, UK
Text by Chris McNab, copyright © 2021 Casemate Publishers

Hardback Edition: ISBN 978-1-63624-086-2
Digital Edition: ISBN 978-1-63624-087-9

A CIP record for this book is available from the British Library

Design by Battlefield Design
Color profiles by Battlefield Design

Printed and bound in Turkey by MegaPrint

For a complete list of Casemate titles, please contact:
CASEMATE PUBLISHERS (US)
Telephone (610) 853-9131
Fax (610) 853-9146
Email: casemate@casematepublishers.com
www.casematepublishers.com

CASEMATE PUBLISHERS (UK)
Telephone (01865) 241249
Email: casemate-uk@casematepublishers.co.uk
www.casematepublishers.co.uk

Facing Title Page: "A fleet of submarines passing H.M.S. Dreadnought," a painting by Charles Edward Dixon in 1909. The ship is in full regalia—for a decade *Dreadnought* served as a powerful ambassador for British interests around the globe.

Title Page: The forward BL 13.5in Mk V guns of HMS *Ajax*, their muzzles plugged with tampions to prevent damage to the bores from sea water.

Contents Page: A head-on view of the dreadnought USS *Texas* (BB-35), showing No. 1 and No. 2 turrets (No. 1 is the lower of the superfiring pair) with the bridge, foremast, and main battery control towering up behind them. (Adam Cuerden); An excellent photograph from the pre-dreadnought *Agamemnon* shows a 12-pounder gun in an anti-aircraft attitude, framed by a rangefinder operator to the left and a searchlight crew to the right.

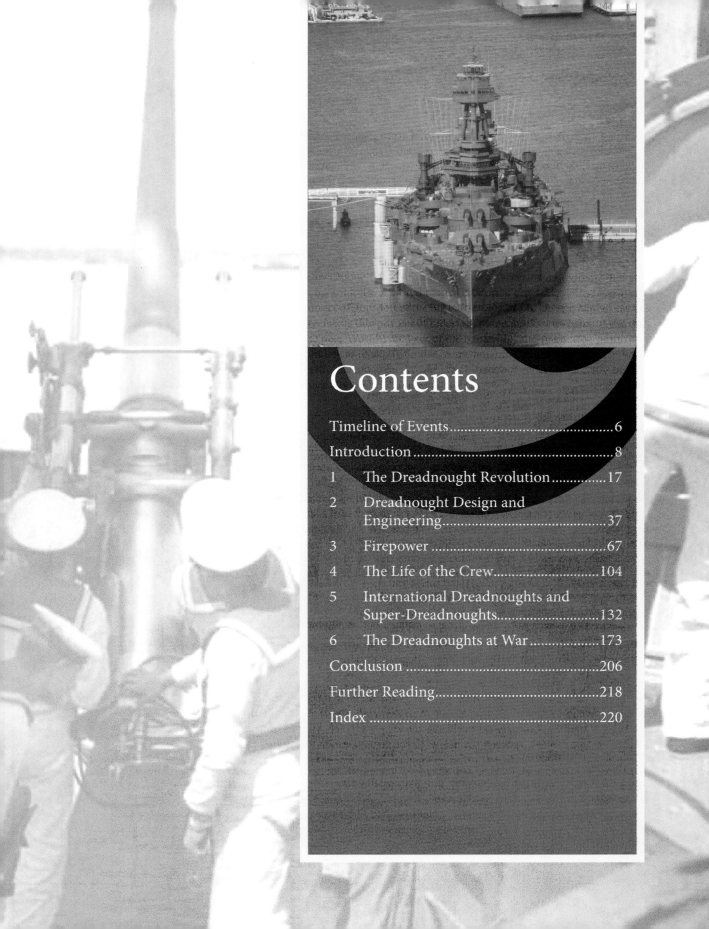

Contents

| Timeline of Events

The evolution of the dreadnoughts and the super-dreadnoughts began with the launch of HMS *Dreadnought* in 1906. The naval arms race that it triggered, however, would run for more than a decade, as the world's navies raced to develop warships of similar, if not greater, capabilities. Yet in hindsight, the race was actually relatively short-lived, as the dreadnoughts and super-dreadnoughts were largely obsolete by the middle of the 1920s, although many of the ships were modernized for service in World War II.

October 2, 1905: HMS *Dreadnought*'s keel is laid down in Portsmouth Dockyard.

February 10, 1906: *Dreadnought* is launched.

December 11, 1906: *Dreadnought* is commissioned into the British fleet.

1907: Germany and Japan begin building their first dreadnoughts, and Brazil orders two dreadnought-class battleships.

1908: Russia begins its dreadnought building program.

1908: The first American dreadnought, USS *South Carolina* (BB-26), is launched on July 11.

1909: Italy lays down its first dreadnought, the *Dante Alighieri.*

1910: Construction begins on the first true French dreadnoughts and Argentina lays down the *Rivadavia* class.

1911: Turkey orders two British-built dreadnoughts, the *Reşadiye* and the *Sultan Osman I*, neither of which is delivered.

August 28, 1914: The battle of Heligoland Bight; the German Navy loses three light cruisers and a torpedo boat.

September 20, 1914: U-boat *U-9* sinks three obsolete Royal Navy cruisers.

November 1, 1914: Action off Coronel, Chile; the British lose two armored cruisers to the *Scharnhorst* and *Gneisenau.*

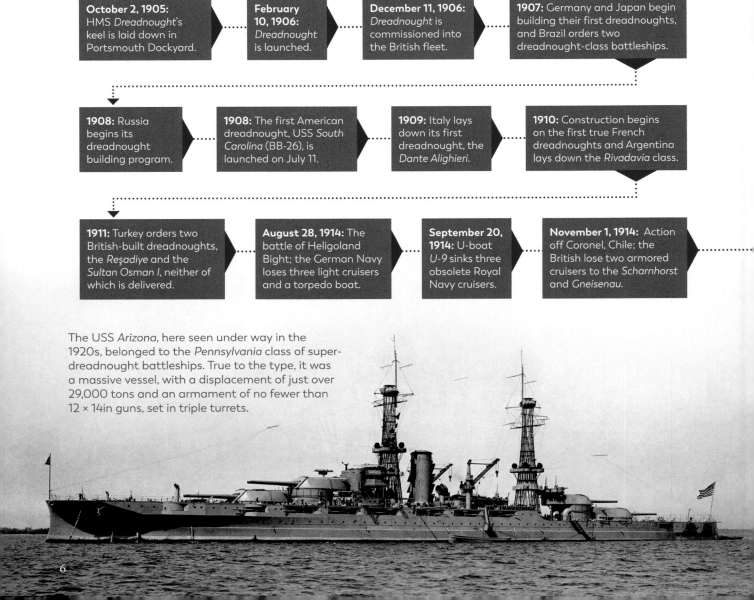

The USS *Arizona*, here seen under way in the 1920s, belonged to the *Pennsylvania* class of super-dreadnought battleships. True to the type, it was a massive vessel, with a displacement of just over 29,000 tons and an armament of no fewer than 12 × 14in guns, set in triple turrets.

HMS *Colossus* was the lead ship in the British *Colossus* class and was laid down in July 1909. We are here looking towards the aft breech-loading (BL) 12in Mk XI guns.

January 24, 1915: The battle of Dogger Bank, a major battlecruiser action with one German ~~battlecruiser~~ lost.
armored cruiser (Blücher)

May 31–June 1, 1916: The battle of Jutland sees the German High Seas Fleet and the British Grand Fleet engage in open battle. Losses are heavy on both sides, although both also declare victory.

November 11, 1918: Allied victory ushers in the Armistice.

February 1919: *Dreadnought* is decommissioned

June 21, 1919: The German High Seas Fleet is scuttled at Scapa Flow.

1946: HMS *Vanguard*, the last battleship in history, is launched.
should be at end of time line

October 14, 1939: *Revenge*-class super-dreadnought *Royal Oak* sunk by U-boat attack at Scapa Flow.

November 25, 1941: *Queen Elizabeth*-class super-dreadnought HMS *Barham* of "Force K" sunk by U-331.

December 7, 1941: Japanese air attack on Pearl Harbor sinks four battleships and damages a further four.

December 10, 1941: HMS *Prince of Wales* and HMS *Repulse* sunk off Malaya by Japanese air attack, the first-time capital warships destroyed by airpower.

HMS *Irresistible* was a *Formidable*-class battleship launched in 1898, and is a fitting representative of the pre-dreadnought type, with a mixed armament of 4 × 12in and 12 × 6in guns, plus 10 × QF (quick-firing) 3-pdr weapons and four torpedo tubes.

Introduction

At the turn of the 20th century, the Royal Navy reigned supreme over the world's oceans. Between 1901 and 1904, for example, the navy boasted no fewer than 45 full-sized battleships in operation, the cream of its fleet, and three in reserve, this force a living testimony to British might in gun and steel. Furthermore, British industrial capacity was at its peak, the shipyards launching ships at a rate against which other nations could not compete. Yet new visions of naval warfare—prompted by lessons learned from recent conflicts—were leading some forward-looking individuals to propose a dramatic change in the primary tools of seaborne battle. Britain's venerable Royal Navy was about to undergo a seismic shift, one that would drag the rest of the world along in its wake.

In the early years of the 20th century, the supreme expression of naval might was the ironclad battleship. Battleships had evolved from the wooden-hulled, steam-and-sail-powered vessels with smoothbore cannon typical of the mid-19th century, through to iron-hulled, armored warships fitted with turreted breech-loading and rifled guns, driven by powerful steam engines. A typical example of such a beast was the British vessel *Irresistible*, one of the three battleships in the *Formidable* class. Laid down in April 1898 and completed in February 1902, the *Irresistible* was 431 feet 8 inches long and had a displacement of 15,000 tons. Power came from two 3-cylinder vertical triple-expansion engines, fueled by 20 Bellville-type water-tube boilers, with the related coal bunkers holding anywhere from 900 to 2,200 tons of coal. Maximum speed was 18 knots (21mph). The warship was wrapped in armor—at its shallowest on the main deck at 1 inch, while bulkhead and barbette armor could thicken up to 12 inches.

Most relevant to our future discussion was its armament. The armament of the "pre-dreadnought" battleships was decidedly mixed, the warship designers covering all their bases with firepower ranging from hefty long-range 12-inch (sometimes 13-inch) guns down to diminutive deck guns used for close-range work. Thus, the *Irresistible* had 4 × 12in 40-caliber Armstrong Whitworth main guns, set in pairs in turrets fore and aft; 12 × 6in Quick-Firing (QF) guns; 16 × 12-pdr QFs; 6 × 3-pdr guns; 4 × 18in torpedo tubes; and two machine guns for good measure.

A peaceful image of the *Formidable*-class battleship HMS *Implacable* anchored at Spithead in 1909, an awning stretched over the rear deck to shield from the sun. The ship is seen here after fire-control platforms were added to its foremast and mainmast.

A painting of Admiral Togo Heihachiro on the bridge of the battleship *Mikasa*, a pre-dreadnought warship that served with distinction as the admiral's flagship during the Russo-Japanese War.

The mixed armament of the pre-dreadnoughts was partly the result of the inadequacies of fire control rather than any mistrust in the capabilities of the individual gun sets. Accurate naval gunnery at range was still rather in its infancy, and while the heaviest guns had capabilities of up to some 15,000 yards, the limitations of fire control meant that the typical maximum combat range was just 2,000 yards. Hence having batteries of smaller guns was a useful insurance policy in case the combat closed quickly to shorter ranges; the more nimble, quick-firing guns—so the thinking went—would be able to smother the target with sheer weight of shot, while the big guns became more cumbersome and less effective against more proximate targets. The lighter guns could also respond more quickly to small, fast attackers. This was not to say that the issue of the correct distribution and weight of firepower was a done deal. In fact, it inspired passionate debate, and opting for a mixed argument was one way to bypass all the arguments and hedge your bets.

The All-big-gun Battleship

The man who dominated the early stages of dreadnought development is John Fisher (1841–1920), one of the landmark figures in the history of the modern Royal Navy. By the turn of the 20th century, Fisher had already been in the navy an astonishing 46 years (he had entered the service in 1854 at the age of 13), and he was appointed First Sea Lord in 1904, a position he held until 1910. During this time, his administrative and organizational vision, plus his deep understanding of the principles and technologies of naval gunnery, helped revolutionize warship design.

With Fisher's ascent to First Sea Lord, he plunged himself into the debate already hinted at—the best design for the navy's capital ships. Essentially, the heat of the debate was generated by two main issues—speed and gunnery. Regarding the tactical merits of speed, there were those who argued that speed was a relative affair,

The *Turbinia* was the first steam turbine-powered steamship, launched in 1894. The powerplant was developed by Charles Algernon Parsons in the 1880s, and although it took time to perfect the system, it offered new levels of efficiency and speed in warship development.

The American pre-dreadnought battleship USS *Texas* (not to be confused with the later dreadnought of the same name) was launched in 1892. Note the heavy defensive citadel amidships and the en echelon arrangement of casemated guns along the hull.

Main gun turrets were en echelon, but casemate guns are symmetrically arranged.

When it came to the critical, indeed defining, issue of the ship's armament, the warship's main armament was provided in the form of 10 × 12in guns. These were arranged in twin turrets as follows: three turrets were set on the centerline—one fore, one aft, and one amidships—with another turret on each beam. Bearing in mind that the wing turrets could also be presented to fire forward, the total fire profile was six guns to the front, eight to each broadside, and six to the rear. Apart from the main guns, the *Dreadnought* was also to be equipped with a secondary anti-torpedo boat armament of 18 × 12-pdrs, while for making torpedo attacks herself the ship had five torpedo tubes below the waterline. (More about the detailed layout of the ship will be explained in the Chapter 2.)

With the *Dreadnought* design finalized and approved by the committee and by the Admiralty, all that now remained was for the ship to be built. Speed was of the essence. The Admiralty was aware that as soon as the ship's properties and qualities were revealed to the global naval community, Britain would be in a race to stay ahead, hence the ships had to go from keel-laying to commission in record time. This goal was indeed achieved, through the spectacular efforts of Thomas Mitchell, the Manager Constructive Department (MCD), plus what would eventually be a total construction workforce of 3,000 men, laboring virtually around the clock. The timings were consequently truly impressive, even in the context of the greatest shipbuilding nation in the world at that time.

HMS *Dreadnought* five days after the hull was laid, with the beginnings of the framework to support the armored deck in place. It took just over four months to take the ship from keel-laying to launch.

Progress continues—a photograph of HMS *Dreadnought* taken 36 days after the keel had been laid. The plating of the armored deck is largely complete and beams for main deck are visible.

The keel was laid down in Portsmouth Dockyard on October 2, 1905, and the ship was launched, with King Edward VII performing the ceremony, on February 10, 1906. On September 29, she received her crew, conducted steam trials over the following two weeks, and a 24-hour acceptance trial on December 1–2. On December 11, the new warship was commissioned into the Special Service Home Fleet and took her full complement of crew. The very next month, *Dreadnought* began a three-month experimental cruise, and was fully revealed to an expectant world.

Countering Criticisms

Any radically different weapon system attracts criticism, and the *Dreadnought* was no exception. The *Dreadnought* seemed to polarize opinion around the world. There were those who regarded the vessel as a triumphant revolution in naval design—one that gave the Royal Navy a formidable lead in the naval arms race. It is common in books and articles on the *Dreadnought* and the dreadnought class to say that the warship rendered all other battleships obsolete. We need to be precise in what we mean by this. Essentially, the advocates of the *Dreadnought* believed that such warships would be able to outgun their opponents at long ranges, effectively destroying them through thunderous weight of 12-inch fire before they had chance bring their own guns or torpedoes to bear. The dreadnoughts would also have the speed to perform rapid battle maneuvers and deployments, faster than foreign ships of equivalent size, and would have the armor to survive battering shellfire exchanges.

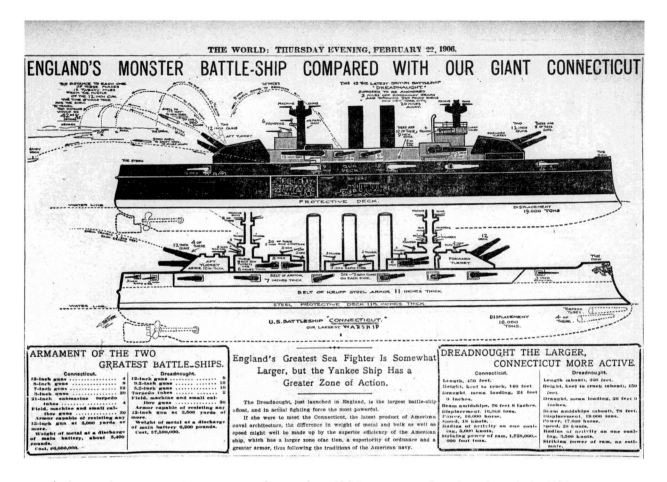

An interesting comparative newspaper feature from 1906, comparing *Dreadnought* with the USS *Connecticut* (BB-18), suggests the impact of *Dreadnought* on naval thinking, although the American author is defiant about the relative capabilities in gunnery.

Yet far from everyone was convinced. American authorities such as Thayer were unimpressed, saying that the slower-firing, heavier guns of the *Dreadnought* would leave it open to being overwhelmed by the more rapid-firing secondary armament of other warships at closer ranges. Sir William Henry White, Chief Constructor of the Admiralty, gave a lecture at the Society of Arts on February 12, 1906, two days after *Dreadnought's* launch, in which he expressed his reservations publicly. *The Times* reported his views as follows:

> The practical abolition of the secondary armament was no new idea and had been a subject of discussion for years; it was really a tendency to return to the state of things that existed in the old DREADNOUGHT, which had four heavy guns and nothing else but very light guns. The argument was that with the very long ranges now unavoidable no gun but the 12in. was worth having; therefore, the proper course was to get rid of all the others, with the concurrent advantage of simplifying the ammunition supply. On the other band, it was an unproved assumption that the 12in. was the only gun worth considering. That penetration was not the only thing shown in the late war, when the Russians declared they were blinded by the Japanese fire from smaller guns. To suggest that one ship with ten 12in. guns would be equal to two or three earlier battleships each carrying four 12in. guns was another

unproved assumption. To judge from published descriptions of the DREADNOUGHT, she had two 12in. guns in a forecastle, with two pairs of the same guns behind; in that case, in the conditions that would give six guns ahead, continuous sighting would be impossible for four of them. Again, the ammunition for these six guns must be massed in a comparatively small longitudinal area. He did not wish to raise objections to the DREADNOUGHT but from what had been published about her it appeared that the desire to increase bow fire and broadside fire in her involved serious drawbacks and left untouched the objections to the omission of a secondary armament.

The Times, February 13, 1906

This was just the tip of the iceberg when it came to the criticisms. They were assailed for being too expensive, not maneuverable enough, of unproven reliability, and vulnerable to attack. An examination of the primary sources from this period reveals numerous Admiralty documents defending the *Dreadnought* from its detractors. Publicly, the Admiralty was rather hamstrung in its defense because they rather wanted to play down the revolutionary nature of the design to allow them to build up a construction lead over competing nations. Whatever the detractors might say, however, there was little denying the fact that the rest of the world quickly bought into the idea of the dreadnought type.

HMS *Dreadnought* at anchor in 1909, three years after its launch. This image provides a good perspective on the armament arrangement, including the two wing turrets ("P" and "Q") set port and starboard of the forward superstructure.

HMS *Dreadnought* under way. During *Dreadnought*'s sea trials in October 1906, the ship reached 21.6 knots (24.9 mph) from 27,018shp.

In Profile:
Admiralty Defence—H.M. Ships
"Dreadnought" and *"Invincible"*

The Admiralty Board document entitled *H.M. Ships "Dreadnought" and "Invincible"* and labelled "Strictly Secret" made a strong defense of the dreadnought type:

> The features of these novel designs which have been most adversely criticized are:

> 1. The uniform 12-inch armament.

> 2. The increase in speed.

> The increase in size and cost due to 1 and 2.

1. *The Armament.*

The papers by the Controller and Director of Naval Ordnance deal with the reasons which led to the adoption of the uniform 12-inch armament argued from the constructors' and gunnery points of view and prove the wisdom of the Admiralty policy of adopting a uniform armament of the heaviest gun in use. A very convincing argument will also be found in the following statement, which is based on the average of the results obtained by the Fleet in the 1905 battle practice: it shows the weight of projectiles in pounds that would hit an enemy (the size of the practice battle target) in 10 minutes if the rapidity and accuracy of fire from a pair of 6-inch, 9.2-inch or 12-inch guns equaled the average obtained in that practice.

HMS *Monarch* was the second of four *Orion*-class dreadnoughts, although, given the fitting of 10 × BL 13.5in Mk V guns and heavier armor, they have also been designated as super-dreadnoughts.

	Weight of projectile (pounds) hitting an enemy in 10 minutes	Relative value
Two 6-inch guns	840	1
Two 9.2-inch guns	2,812	3.3
Two 12-inch guns	4,250	5

The great superiority of the 12-inch gun is shown at this range, which was a little under 6,000 yards, and is less than the probable mean battle range; the figures are proportionately in favor of the lighter gun.

2. *The Increase in Speed.*

It is admitted that strategically speed is of very great importance. It enables the fleet or fleets possessing it to concentrate at any desired spot as quickly as possible, and it must therefore exercise an important influence on the course of a naval war, rapid concentration being one of the chief factors of success.

But it is often contended that tactically speed is of little value, although it gives the choice range and enables the disposition, or line of bearing, of a fleet to be rapidly changed. The fact is often overlooked that high speed is a necessity now that long range hitting is possible, for the greater the distance between the opposing line in a fleet action the greater the space to be traversed in order to *gain* or *maintain* a commanding position with respect to the enemy's line.

3. *Size and Cost.*

In both these respects the 'Dreadnought' compares favorably with the battleships projected by the foreign Powers, and it may be stated that of the four next naval powers to Britain, two propose building ships of equal size and cost, and two of greater size and greater cost.

The 'Invincibles' are larger and more costly than other armored cruisers to be built by foreign Powers, but the speed of the latter is inferior to that of many of the cruisers already afloat, and such vessels would be little use attached to a fleet of 'Dreadnoughts', whereas the three 'Invincibles', with their fine speed and great gun power, will ensure an unwilling enemy being brought to action, or should the enemy be anxious to fight, they will be able to select the most advantageous position from which to attack the enemy and support the Battle Fleet.

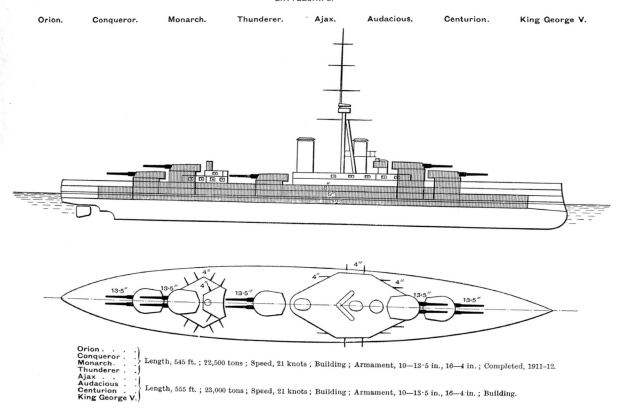

BATTLESHIPS.

Orion.　Conqueror.　Monarch.　Thunderer.　Ajax.　Audacious,　Centurion.　King George V.

Orion .
Conqueror .
Monarch .
Thunderer .
⟩ Length, 545 ft.; 22,500 tons; Speed, 21 knots; Building; Armament, 10—13·5 in., 16—4 in.; Completed, 1911-12.

Ajax .
Audacious .
Centurion .
King George V.
⟩ Length, 555 ft.; 23,000 tons; Speed, 21 knots; Building; Armament, 10—13·5 in., 16—4 in.; Building.

Layout plans of British dreadnoughts from *The Naval Annual 1913*, showing how the firepower of British capital warships had gravitated to the centerline by the *Orion* and *King George V* classes.

The Effect

Once *Dreadnought* was released to the world's view, there was also a curiously positive type of problem for the British. *Dreadnought* posed a strategic threat. In 1906, the Royal Navy had an undoubted numerical superiority in warships, and one that could be maintained by British shipbuilding capacity. By launching a new type of ship that rendered all previous battleship designs obsolete, Britain was intentionally creating a level playing field, which given the industrial might emerging in countries such as Germany and the United States, it could potentially lose.

The Admiralty, and eventually the British public, however, swung squarely behind the dreadnought building program, pumping millions of pounds and man hours into outstripping the rivals, especially once a startled Germany entered the naval arms race in earnest. (A more detailed study of the international development of the dreadnoughts and super-dreadnoughts is given in Chapter 5.)

It was an arms race that Britain won, or at least did so by the outbreak of World War I. Official British tables of ship production published around 1910 proudly declared that the average contract production time for a dreadnought battleship was 24 months, as opposed to the 36 months it took for Germany to produce a similar vessel. So it was, that between 1906 and 1914, Britain manufactured and commissioned no fewer than 29 dreadnought or super-dreadnoughts (the latter is explained below), against the output of 17 vessels by the Germans. By 1920, which is effectively when the dreadnought type ceased to be made in Britain, a total of 35 of these great vessels had graced the waves. Naval historian Angus Konstam points out that this Herculean shipbuilding effort cost the British nation a total of £151 million.

GREAT BRITAIN.

BATTLESHIPS.

Formidable. *Bulwark. Implacable. Irresistible. *London.
    *Prince of Wales. *Queen. *Venerable.

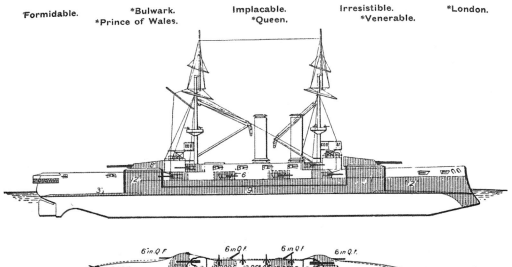

ˣ In These Ships 9″ Armour Tapers to 2″ at
30 ft From Bow, & They Have no Forward
Bulkhead

Length, 400 ft. ; 15,000 tons ; Speed, 18—18·3 knots ; Completed, 1901–1904 ;
Armament, 4—12 in., 12—6 in., 18—12 pr., 8 small.

See page 217.

Canopus. Albion. Glory. Goliath. Ocean. Vengeance.

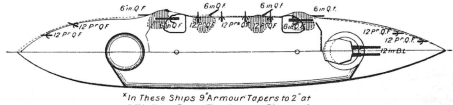

Length, 390 ft. ; 12,950 tons ; Speed, 18·2—18·5 knots ; Completed, 1900–1902 ;
Armament, 4—12 in., 12—6 in., 12—12 pr., 8 small.

See page 215.

The *Formidable* and *Canopus* classes of pre-dreadnought stayed in Royal Navy service until the end of
World War I, despite being severely outdated. These plan views show the heavy proliferation of 6-inch
QF guns around the hulls.

Battlecruisers
launched (prewar)
ie. before
Aug 1914
British
1. Invincible
2. Inflexible
3. Indomitable
4. Indefatigable
5. Australia
6. New Zealand
7. Lion
8. Princess Royal
9. Queen Mary
10. Tiger
German
1. Von der Tann
2. Moltke
3. Goeben
4. Seydlitz
5. Derfflinger
6. Lützow
Hindenburg would not
be launched until 1915

Nor were the dreadnoughts the only focus of the British naval output during these epic years. Running adjacent to the battleship building was also the development of the new "battlecruiser" type. The battlecruiser was also conceived, from 1904, as an "all-big-gun" warship so that it could trade shells at long range with the biggest enemy vessels. Yet unlike the dreadnoughts, the battlecruisers were to have less-substantial armor, the trade-off being the speed required to deploy quickly and decisively to trouble spots as they flared up. Thus, while the *Dreadnought* had 11 inches belt armor and a speed of 21 knots, the *Invincible*—the lead ship of the *Invincible* class of battlecruisers (*Invincible, Indomitable, Inflexible*)—had just 6 inches of belt armor but a top speed of more than 25 knots, even while carrying a main armament of 10×12in guns. Fisher became highly invested in the battlecruiser type, even seeing it as superior to the dreadnoughts. Indeed, the large battlecruisers that emerged over the next 20 years often had little to distinguish them from the dreadnoughts in power and dimensions. Thus, to the prewar British output of 29 dreadnoughts, we should also add nine battlecruisers, although in this field the margin of superiority compared to the Germans was slimmer—Tirpitz's navy launched seven battlecruisers during the same period. *Incorrect - British had 10 battlecruisers launched vs Germans six (see left)*

The dreadnought was a true game-changer, a warship that affected the very strategic composition of the global powers. Yet before we go on to analyze the evolution of the British dreadnought type, we should stop and revisit, for a moment, the classic claim that the dreadnought rendered all other warships obsolete. A useful

A fine view of *Dreadnought* under sail, the photograph likely taken during the ship's steam trials in 1906, as the ship does not have the 24-inch searchlight that was fitted under the foretop on the main mast in October/November 1906.

lens through which to view this debate is a British newspaper report from *The Times*, published on July 18, 1910, and squarely titled "What is a Dreadnought?" Given that the public was now aware of just how much of their economy was being poured into these hulking vessels, the newspaper obviously felt that some technical clarification was needed. The article also provides a useful window on what other nations were doing at the same time:

> If we look in another direction, it might perhaps at first sight appear as if the distinctive feature of a Dreadnought consisted in her being equipped with an armament of what in American phraseology is termed the 'all-big-gun single-calibre' type. That was no doubt the true differentia of the original Dreadnought, which is armed for the purposes of a fleet action with ten 12-inch guns and no others, her remaining armament of twenty-four 12-pounder guns being intended only for defense against torpedo attack. It is also the true differentia of the later British Dreadnoughts, though in their case the anti-torpedo armament is of larger caliber. But it is not the true differentia of many of the more recent so-called Dreadnoughts built or building for foreign Navies. The French Danton class is to carry four 12-inch and twelve 9.4-inch guns, thus approximating very closely to our own Lord Nelson type, which is armed with four 12-inch and ten 9.2-inch guns, together in each case with a powerful anti-torpedo armament. The German Nassau type carries twelve 11-inch and twelve 5.9-inch guns, together with an additional anti-torpedo armament. The armament of the projected Italian Dreadnoughts is not given in the Dilke Return [an annual statement of serviceable warships, named after its moving force, Sir Charles Dilke] and though some details are furnished in the 'Naval Annual,' they are there stated to be uncertain. In the United States the Delaware type now completed is armed with ten 12-inch and fourteen 5-inch guns, together with an anti-torpedo armament, though it may be that the 5-inch armament is intended mainly for defense against torpedo attack. The Florida and Arkansas types now building are similarly but more powerfully armed. The Japanese ships of the Kawachi type are to carry twelve 12-inch, ten 6-inch, and fourteen 4–7-inch guns, the latter no doubt for defense against torpedo attack. Russia alone of the Powers enumerated in the Dilke Return appears to approximate in the ships of the Sevastopol type to the original Dreadnought differentia, since these ships are to be armed with twelve 12-inch and twelve 4–7-inch guns, together with an additional anti-torpedo armament of a lighter character. It is clear, then, from this enumeration that the 'all-big-gun single-caliber' armament is not a true and distinctive differentia of many of the so-called Dreadnoughts now built and building by the leading naval Powers of the world. Such an armament is to be found in some of them, but not in all, and apparently not in the majority …
>
> In other words, when we speak of a Dreadnought nowadays, we mean nothing more than a warship of the first class which has been designed and constructed at some time posterior to the year 1906. All such ships are no doubt somewhat faster, in many cases much faster, much more heavily armed, and of larger displacement, in many cases of much larger displacement, than the 'capital ships' still fit to lie in a line which immediately preceded them; but development in these several directions is only in the natural order of evolution—an order of evolution which has been more or less continuous ever since the first ironclad was constructed—and does not itself constitute a differentia which separates the original Dreadnought and all 'capital ships' since constructed from all those which preceded her. It may thus very well be held that the growing habit of talking about Dreadnoughts only, and thinking in Dreadnoughts only, is not unlikely to lead to much confusion in the public mind, and even to some confusion in naval policy.

This is a subtle and sophisticated argument. The writer explains how the dreadnoughts are, in real material terms, evolutions of the battleship design, not an actual revolution. Furthermore, he also exposes how the all-big-gun concept was not watertight, especially when looking at developments farther afield, where the secondary armament remained robust. Indeed, if we look closely at the continual development of the British dreadnought, we do detect a shifting movement in philosophy from 1906 onwards.

From *Dreadnought* to Super-Dreadnoughts

HMS *Bellerophon* was the lead ship of its class and was launched on July 27, 1907. In 1913/14 the two 4-inch guns atop the forward turret were moved and mounted on the superstructure.

As noted, having leveled the playing field with the launch of *Dreadnought*, the priority for the Admiralty was then to maintain the momentum of the initial lead with a continuous, high-tempo shipbuilding program. This it did immediately with the development of the *Bellerophon* class of dreadnoughts, three vessels (*Bellerophon*, *Superb*, and *Temeraire*) that were largely identical models of the benchmark ship, with some key differences. The first of these ships was laid down on December 3, 1906, and the last of them was completed, ready for service, in May 1909. But this was just the beginning. Between 1907 and 1914, two more classes of dreadnought were completed—the *St Vincent* class (*Collingwood*, *St Vincent*, and *Vanguard*), the *Colossus* class (*Colossus* and *Hercules*), plus two independent battleships of the series (*Neptune* and *Agincourt*). Although the timescale of production was particularly rapid, the dreadnought warships nevertheless underwent a significant series of changes. The layout of the main armament on deck was radically revised, shifting towards a centerline-only, fore, and aft superfiring arrangement of the main guns, rather than having the dual wing and amidships turrets. The

A long view down the port side of the dreadnought HMS *Colossus*, showing the diagonal torpedo net spars running along the side.

The *Invincible*-class battlecruiser HMS *Inflexible* anchored at Spithead for the Naval Review in June 1909. Reviews provided the opportunity for major fleet exercises as well as the opportunity to demonstrate naval power.

secondary battery, the omission of which formed the grounding rationale for the original *Dreadnought*, steadily crept back in, both in response to tactical considerations and also through acknowledging the developments in rival foreign dreadnought vessels. Superstructure arrangements changed accordingly, and also in the attempt to provide a better observation platform for the gunnery spotting top, up high on the foremast.

Warships such as the *Revenge*-class HMS *Ramillies* seen here represent a later vision of the British super-dreadnought, with massive firepower—the same 10 × BL 15in Mk I guns, but with increased armored protection compared to the preceding *Queen Elizabeth* class.

8 not 10 15" guns

Such adjustments helped keep the British dreadnoughts in the line of battle, but once the arms race was under way, speed of production was far from the only consideration that came into play. Any arms race forms the ideal conditions for technological advancement, and the pre-1914 naval competition was no exception. For towards the end of the first decade of the 20th century, the British Admiralty began to receive intelligence about the gunnery formats of rival dreadnought designs. More specifically, there was evidence that the American, Japanese and, most worryingly, German navies were looking into the possibility of mounting main guns of a caliber larger than 12 inches—specifically 13.5-inch, 14-inch, and 15-in calibers. These offered greater range, more destructive capability, a flatter trajectory, and therefore improved accuracy and fire control.

This painting by William Lionel Wyllie is a study of *Iron Duke*-class battleship at anchor in 1918. Note how the vessel is fitted with an aircraft flying-off platform on B turret, just forward of the bridge.

Picking up on the first rumblings of at least some of these developments around 1909, the British knew that the dreadnought needed an upgrade if it was to face the future threats. The result was the series of ships we label as "super-dreadnoughts," and their production began with the *Orion* class (*Conqueror, Monarch, Orion,* and *Thunderer*) as part of the 1909 shipbuilding program. Gone were the days of the wing turrets; these ships each had 10–13.5in Mk V guns all mounted on the centerline, with "B" (fore) and "X" (aft) turrets superimposed over the "A" and "Y" turrets respectively. The *Orions* were also more substantial vessels than the preceding *Colossus* class of dreadnoughts. They were longer, with a displacement increase of more than 2,000 tons, plus they had some armor increases. The British super-dreadnoughts had arrived.

There would be a total of five classes of British super-dreadnought—*Orion, King George V, Iron Duke, Queen Elizabeth,* and *Royal Sovereign*—which together constituted 22 vessels, plus two privately built warships, HMS *Erin* and HMS *Canada*. The super-dreadnoughts were naked expressions of force, and with the launch and commissioning of each new class, they grew in power, size, and destructive potential. Again, the details of this development are explored in more detail in later chapters, but it is worth mentioning some notable landmarks.

In the *Iron Duke* class, launched in 1912–13, the secondary armament was upped to 6-inch guns, replacing the 4-inch QF guns of previous dreadnoughts and super-dreadnoughts. The move was rational—the increased threat of smaller vessels such as destroyers, light cruisers, and fast torpedo boats meant that the secondary armament now had more of a role to play—but it essentially signaled the end of the dreadnought-type vessel as

HMS *Vanguard* seen just after her launch on February 22, 1909. *Vanguard* had a violent accidental end, destroyed by magazine explosions on July 9, 1917, at Scapa Flow, killing almost all of the ship's 845 crew.

This photograph, taken in 1945, shows the battlecruiser HMS *Renown* after nearly three decades of modernization and upgrades. As the lead ship of the *Renown* class, she had an extraordinary as-built top speed of 32 knots (37mph).

an "all-big-gun" design. This move faced little resistance, not least because Fisher had retired in 1910. Not that the focus on big guns had dimmed. With the news about American and Japanese naval gunnery developments, the DNO decided to fit the *Queen Elizabeth* class with the new 15-in Mk I BL (breech-loading) guns, some eight of these monsters in total. The *Royal Sovereign* class also adopted this firepower. It cannot have been anything other than awe-inspiring to witness a broadside ripping out one of these great vessels.

The super-dreadnoughts were the apotheosis of a new generation of vessels that had first run down the slipways in 1906. Since the launch of *Dreadnought*, the battleships of Britain and the other major international naval players had grown immensely in size and power, their massive silhouettes and brooding gunnery suggesting that nothing could challenge their authority. This was not to be the case.

Another example of a dreadnought under construction, this time the *Sultan Osman I*, a ship that Brazil originally ordered in 1911 as the *Rio de Janeiro* from Armstrong Whitworth but which Brazil later sold to Turkey. The ship never reached the Ottomans and became instead HMS *Agincourt*.

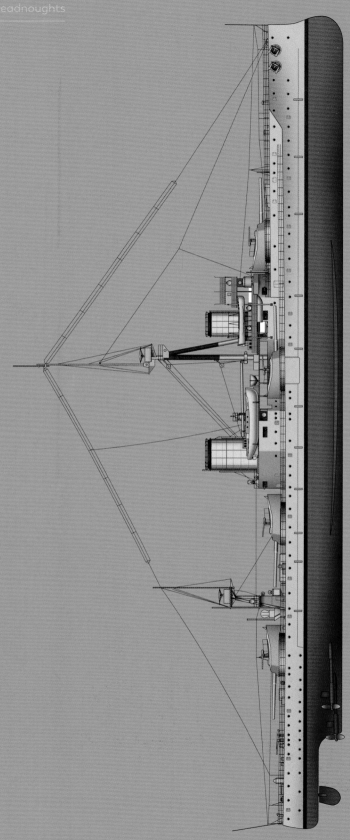

In Profile: *Dreadnought*

2
Dreadnought Design and Engineering

The dreadnoughts were living communities afloat. The layout of each ship had to facilitate not only the violence of naval combat, but also the daily processes that enabled the ship to perform countless more mundane duties at home and abroad. To get a sense of how dreadnoughts and super-dreadnoughts were structurally organized in general, we need to go back to the grandfather of them all—the original *Dreadnought*. By describing how this seminal ship was designed, we are better placed to understand the thinking behind the many subsequent changes and design upgrades implemented between 1906 and the early 1920s.

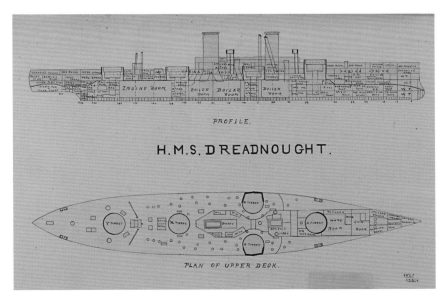

A basic plan of HMS *Dreadnought* as built. Note the positioning of the "P" and "Q" wing turrets, with their necessarily limited traverse. Note the volume of internal space taken by boiler rooms. (© National Maritime Museum, Greenwich, London)

Some basic data about the *Dreadnought* gives us context. The overall length of the warship was 526 feet, the length between perpendiculars was 490 feet, and the ship's beam was 82 feet. With a normal load, the battleship's displacement was 17,110 tons, but at maximum load that figure rose to 21,845 tons. At normal load, the draught was 28 feet, rising to 29 feet for deep loading.

Dreadnought was intended for high performance, and its hull structure reflected that priority. Looking at the ship in transverse profile, we see that it had a very square profile amidships, with a flat bottom and near vertical sides, much like that found on the earlier *Lord Nelson* class of pre-dreadnought vessel. This type of hull form was good for enabling the ship to handle its displacement with a stable sea performance, reducing the level of roll. However, flat-bottomed boats have an increased drag, the compensation for which came in the design of *Dreadnought*'s stern and bow. At the bow, particular attention was paid to the design of the stem (the underwater projection from the bow). The stem derived from the ram fitted to an earlier generation of ships, but by 1906 ramming was a rare tactic indeed, except when used against much lighter, smaller and more fragile vessels. However, the stem had the ancillary benefit of reducing the bow wave, and therefore reducing drag, thus *Dreadnought* was fitted with a smoothly curved profile. To improve the ship's maneuverability, and to provide space for the propellers and rudder, the stern featured a long cut-up.

Another feature of *Dreadnought*'s hull design was its double bottom. This not only provided the ship with greater survivability in case of underwater damage, it also provided a cellular space for the bulk storage of oil. The issue of survivability in the age of big-gun and torpedo warfare was naturally uppermost in the minds of Watts and others as the ship was designed. Beneath the main deck, the ship was divided by a network of longitudinal and transverse bulkheads, these featuring 8-inch armor to the aft bulkhead, protecting vital features such as the shell rooms and magazines. Watertight doors in many of the bulkheads could be swung shut to contain flooding.

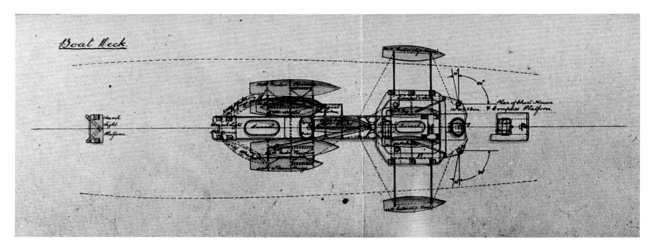

An original drawing of *Dreadnought*'s boat deck, showing the tight arrangement of the small craft between and around the two funnels. (© National Maritime Museum, Greenwich, London)

The issue of armored protection was a complicated one back in 1906, and in some areas of military development remains so to this day. The essential problem is that the more armor is applied, the heavier and slower the ship. So, any ship design was essentially a trade-off between speed (in itself a key ingredient of protection) and armored protection. The distribution of *Dreadnought*'s armor by weight were as follows:

Side armor	1,940 tons
Decks, gratings	1,350 tons

Magazines	250 tons
Steering gear compartment	100 tons
Barbettes	1,260 tons
Bridge	100 tons

These figures are interesting, especially when held in comparison with the pre-dreadnought *Lord Nelson* class of warships. Only in deck/grating and barbette armor do the weight figures exceed those of *Lord Nelson*, despite the fact that *Lord Nelson* was a smaller and lighter ship, which might lead us to conclude that *Dreadnought* was in fact under-armored. The picture defies a simplistic conclusion, however. In terms of the side protection, *Dreadnought* had some vulnerabilities. The side armor consisted of an 11-inch main belt, protecting the ship's machinery from torpedo attack or a low shell-strike, with 8-inch armor over the rest of the ship's sides. However, depending on the loading and therefore displacement of the ship, the main belt generally sat either on or below the waterline, leaving the vessel above the waterline with limited protection, especially from plunging fire.

In terms of the armor applied to other parts of the ship, the following depths applied:

Barbettes	11/8/4in
Turrets	11in sides/13in back/3in roof
Conning tower	11in sides/ 4in floor/3in roof
Signal tower	8in sides/4in floor/3in roof
Main deck	0.75in
Middle deck	1.75–3in (thickest armor over "A" and "Y" magazines)
Lower deck	1.5–4in (4in armor around "A" and "Y" barbettes/3in armor over steering gear)

We can note from these figures that *Dreadnought* was indeed most vulnerable to enemy plunging fire, given that its deck armor was the lightest of all its armor plate. Again, it would take the hard lessons of combat to educate the Admiralty about the need for more resilient deck armor.

Superstructure

Looking broadly at the externals of *Dreadnought*, the first major feature that we encounter working back down the ship from the bow (having passed the three hawse pipes for the anchor chain plus ground tackle, and two 12-inch guns on the starboard side) is the "A" turret, housing twin 12-inch guns. This turret was one of five on *Dreadnought*—there were a further two set on the beams—"P" barbette on the port and "Q" barbette on the starboard—and two rearward-facing barbettes on the centerline consisting of "X" barbette just behind the aft funnel and "Y" barbette overlooking the stern (aft deck). The twenty-four 12-pounder guns were dotted around the forecastle deck and upper deck.

Returning to the front of the ship, directly behind "A" barbette was the elevated bridge and conning tower, and key command spaces such as the navigating platform, chart house, and compass platform. Viewed from any distance, the other most salient features of the ship were the two masts. The foremast, set a short (and ultimately problematic) distance behind the forward funnel, was a tripod structure, with internal ladders within each strut to enable ascent to the searchlight platform and the rangefinder equipped foretop. The shorter mainmast was located to the rear of the aft funnel, and featured searchlight mountings and an elevated main top. Between these two poles another structure worth noting, located on the boat deck, was the signal tower, atop which was fitted another 9 feet Barr & Stroud rangefinder.

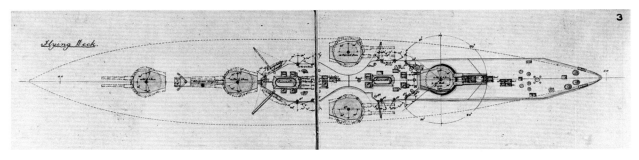

Dreadnought's flying (forecastle) deck, the plan showing both the position of the main armament, plus the range of traverse for the forward 12-inch turret. (© National Maritime Museum, Greenwich, London)

On the boat deck, somewhere obviously had to be found for the small craft. Here was something of a problem for the designers. Generally speaking, the *Dreadnought* was a rather claustrophobic design, by virtue of the locations of "P" and "Q" barbettes, which squeezed the superstructure inwards at the middle. There was also the blast to be considered. If these guns were fired, especially along a line that ranged close to parallel with the ship's sides, blast damage would occur to surrounding structures, hence the superstructure around the gun muzzles had to be pared back to the minimum. The boats also had to be placed intelligently to avoid blast damage. There were eight boats in total clustered around the deck on derrick mounts. To the front of the deck there were two 32-ft cutters (one either side), and a further 32-ft cutter or 27-ft whaler set just behind the foremast. Around the rear funnel and signal tower were six further boats—(1) a 16-ft dinghy, (2) 27-ft whaler, (3) 45-ft steam pinnace, (4) 40-ft steam barge (for the admiral's personal use), (5) 13-ft 6-in balsa raft, and (6) either a 42-ft launch, 36-ft pinnace, or 27-ft whaler.

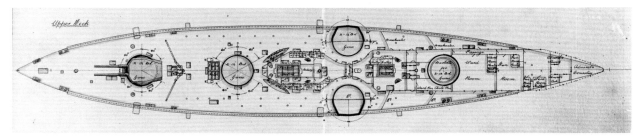

Dreadnought's upper deck plan. The front of the deck is dominated by officers' spaces, including cabins for the admiral's stewards and cooks. (© National Maritime Museum, Greenwich, London)

The rear forecastle and upper decks of the ship were largely given over to the big guns of "X" and "Y" turrets, twin 12-inch guns mounted in each turret. This part of the ship also had a liberal sprinkling of 12-pounder guns including, originally, two atop each of the main gun turrets plus three set farther back on the upper deck, as guardians over the stern. The guns set on the turrets were eventually removed, it being discovered that the blast of the main guns in action was detrimental to both the 12-pounder guns and their crews.

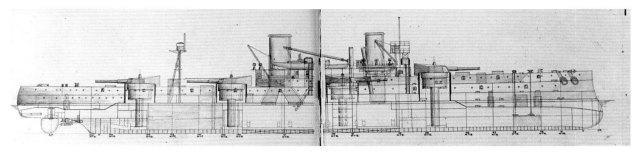

This profile image of *Dreadnought* (from a booklet showing its age) illustrates how the main gun turret ammunition machinery descended almost the full depth of the hull. (© National Maritime Museum, Greenwich, London)

Below Decks

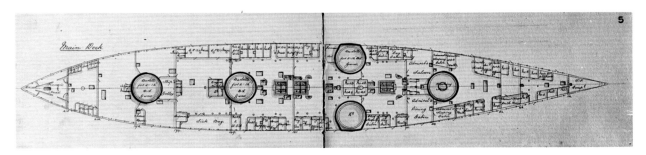

Working down lower into *Dreadnought*, the plan here is of the main deck. Along the sides of this deck, we find most of the senior officers' accommodation. (© National Maritime Museum, Greenwich, London)

Dreadnought was divided into seven deck levels:

- Flying (forecastle) deck
- Upper deck
- Main deck
- Middle deck
- Lower deck
- Platform deck
- Hold

As we descend deeper into the ship, we find a steady transition in purpose from accommodation (mainly concentrated in the upper and main decks) to victualling, engineering, and weaponry. Although the middle deck contained some accommodation aft, including the petty officers' mess, there was a definite emphasis on more practical spaces. There were numerous stores—for paint, engineering equipment, mechanical spares, food (this deck and the lower deck contained refrigeration machinery), cables, diving gear, and gunnery tools—plus engineers' and armorers' workshops (as well as many associated washrooms). Just forward and starboard of "A" barbette was the chart and chronometer room, and next door aft was the torpedo lobby. There were also equipment and hoists to support the functioning of the 12-pounder guns. Coal bunkers were distributed across much of the port and starboard sides.

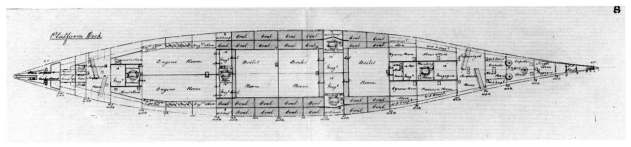

Dreadnought's platform deck plan also shows the position and angling of the four torpedo tubes—two aft and two forward. Magazines for both the 12-inch and 12-pounder guns are at this level. (© National Maritime Museum, Greenwich, London)

Moving down to the lower deck and the platform deck, now the focus of the ship shifted distinctly to its powerplant and to its warfighting role. Dominating these decks were three massive spaces—two boiler rooms and then, in the rear half of the ship, the engine room, with the dynamo space set above the boiler rooms. As these decks were now below the waterline, they were also used extensively for ammunition storage and handling. On the upper deck were working spaces for both 12-inch and 12-pounder ammunition, and associated hoists, plus a torpedo lobby. On the platform deck were the four torpedo tubes (two aft, two forward) and their torpedo rooms (there was another torpedo tube in the stern), plus the 12-inch and 12-pounder magazines and, set in four locations along the length of the ship, airtight cases for storing bagged cordite charges. There was also a small-arms magazine.

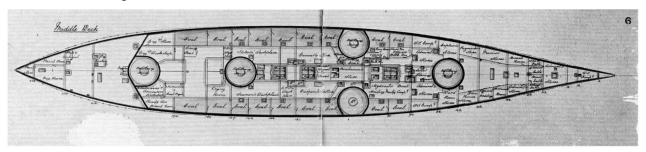

The middle deck, which was more utilitarian in purpose than the decks above. Note the extent of space required for coal. (© National Maritime Museum, Greenwich, London)

Finally, we get to the bottom of the ship, into the hull. Here were the lowermost sections of the boiler room and the engine room, and from the latter ran the four housings that held the propeller shafts. Again, there was ammunition storage and handling facilities—a lower magazine for both the 12-pounder and 12-inch guns, shell rooms for the individual turrets and there was even a store for anti-submarine mines. But the hold was also used for the storage of perishable items such as olive oil, flour, bread and other provisions.

We have taken an overview tour of *Dreadnought* as she appeared in 1907. Naturally, this was just the beginning of her service life, and ahead of her was a seemingly endless series of modifications, refits, and adjustments to keep her relevant and fighting fit. Rather than chart all these modifications in turn, however, it is more historically useful to look at how the British dreadnoughts and super-dreadnoughts began to evolve as types.

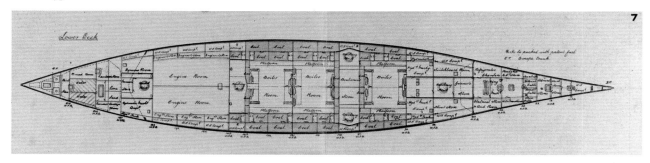

Once we reach *Dreadnought*'s lower deck, seen here, engine rooms and boiler spaces dominate. On this deck we also find the working spaces for the 12-inch ammunition. (© National Maritime Museum, Greenwich, London)

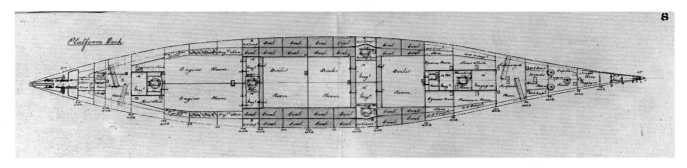

The hold. Note the positioning of the shell rooms—the ammunition hoist trunking ran directly up from here to feed the turrets above. (© National Maritime Museum, Greenwich, London)

From *Bellerophon* to *Vanguard*

As noted, the Admiralty realized that if Britain was to maintain its strategic lead internationally, it had to produce the dreadnoughts rapidly. For this reason, the first class of dreadnoughts to appear—the *Bellerophon* class—was little modified from the progenitor warship. There were some incremental changes, however. A problem of the *Dreadnought* was that the smoke from the forward funnel often rose and swirled around the foremast, obscuring the all-important view of those in the foretop position, with their responsibilities for range-finding and gunnery control. The *Bellerophon* class attempted to remedy this problem by shifting the tripod foremast in front of the funnel, rather than behind as in the *Dreadnought*, but the problem of smoke remained persistent. There were other changes. The slightly different design meant that the class's armor was somewhat thinner than *Dreadnought*'s, attaining a maximum of 10 inches around the belt. By way of protective compensation, the *Bellerophon* vessels had watertight bulkheads running the entire length of the ship; on the *Dreadnought* only, the magazines were given flood protection. But most interesting was the addition of a significant secondary armament, in the form of 16 × 4in QF guns, although this number was reduced with the eventual removal of the guns that were super-mounted atop the 12-inch gun turrets—an impractical location if ever there was.

Three *Bellerophon* warships were laid down and built in 1906/7: *Bellerophon*, *Superb*, and *Temeraire*. They were quickly followed by three more of the *St Vincent* class (*Collingwood*, *St Vincent*, and *Vanguard*), launched between November 7, 1908, and February 22, 1909, with all completed and in service by April 1910. Considering that these were laid down between February 1907 and April 1908, it is evident that the British shipyards were getting into the swing of producing dreadnoughts at breathtaking speed. The principal builders for these craft were Portsmouth Dockyard, Devonport Dockyard, Vickers at Barrow-in-Furness, and Elswick in Tyneside. Although in most ways the *St Vincent* class replicated the previous dreadnought vessels, there were some important changes. The biggest was a change in the armament. The main guns on the previous dreadnoughts—the 45-caliber-long Mk X guns—were replaced with the 50-caliber Mk XI guns, the new guns theoretically offering increased muzzle velocity and therefore a greater range and flatter trajectory. As Chapter 3 outlines, these benefits were not realized fully in reality. Moreover, the addition of the longer, heavier guns meant that the ship had to be stretched in length by about 10 feet (to 536 feet overall), with a slight increase in beam and a slight decrease in draught. Also, while the *Bellerophon* class had a displacement of 18,600 tons, the *St Vincent* vessels were at 19,700 tons (normal load). Not only was the weight of the vessel increased by the modifications in the main armament, but the warship also had an additional four 4in QF guns, making a total of 20. Two of these guns were removed by 1916—those mounted atop "A" and "B" turrets.

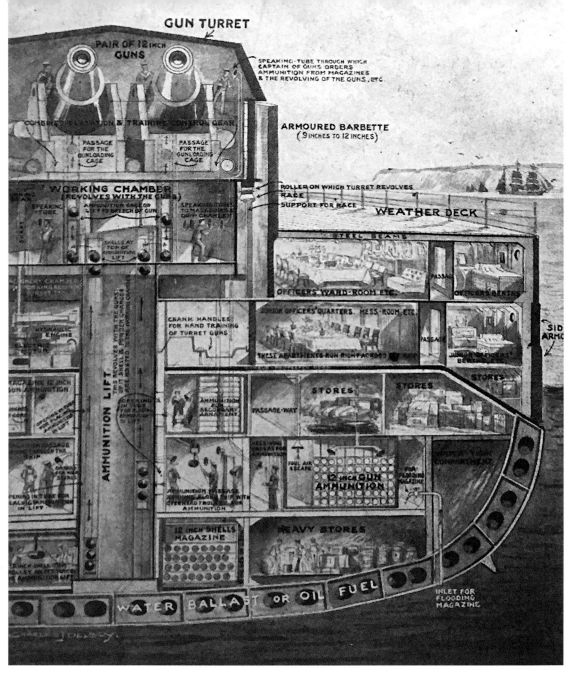

This simplified diagram from *The Wonder Book of the Navy* (4th edition) in the 1920s usefully illustrates gunnery procedures and spaces, showing how shells transitioned from the magazines to the turrets via the ammunition lift.

This twisted chunk of armor came from SMS *Moltke*, hit four times by 15-inch shells during the battle of Jutland. The armor was on display at the Militärhistorisches Museum der Bundeswehr in Dresden (Nick-D)

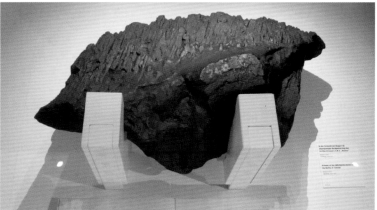

Following *Dreadnought*, the *Bellerophon* and *St Vincent* classes of warship had brought little substantial change to the overall layout of the new British battleship. Herein lay a risk, particularly in the configuration of the armament. The British had watched with interest as the Americans produced their *South Carolina* class of dreadnoughts, the lead ship of the class laid down on December 18, 1906 and completed on March 1, 1910. What made the *South Carolina* truly notable was that it was the first battleship with superfiring turrets both fore and aft—the innermost turret of each pair was raised so that it could fire directly over the top of the turret in front. This invention, courtesy of Chief Constructor Washington L. Capps, transformed battleship firepower. Not only were there space savings to be had from the design, but it also meant that four guns (the *South Carolina* had 8 × 12in guns set in turreted pairs) could engage targets directly ahead or behind at the same time, or all eight guns could be swiveled to deliver a full broadside.

Neptune and the *Colossus* Class

The British sat up and took notice, but at first only partially with the development and launch of HMS *Neptune*. Actually, the British were already getting some experience of building battleships with superfiring turrets. A Brazilian order for two dreadnought-type battleships, designed to counter Argentinian naval expansion, featured superfiring turrets fore and aft, plus the usual wing turrets of the earlier British dreadnoughts. This order, fulfilled by Armstrong and Vickers, gave the British a technical understanding of the superfiring configuration, which they then applied to *Neptune*.

HMS *Dreadnought* viewed from the starboard side. With a deep load the warship had a draught of 29 feet 7.5 inches.

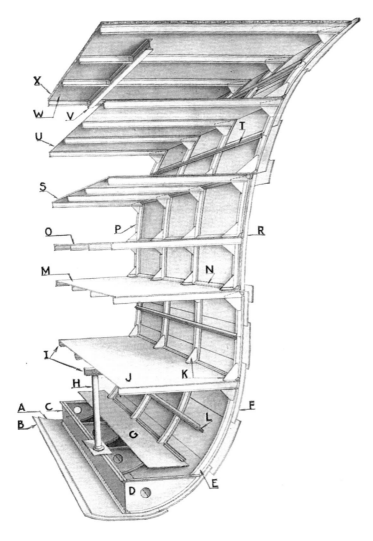

Royal Sovereign's midship section, showing the deck structure and the secondary hull structure.

that comprised the secondary armament were set back more amidships, to avoid the flooding problems of the gunnery positions of earlier classes. The ships' metacentric height was lowered, to enhance the steadiness required for accurate shooting. A notable feature of the superstructure was that there was only one funnel, with the high foretop well out of the reach of the funnel's smoke emissions.

The *Royal Sovereign* class was the last of the major classes of super-dreadnoughts to be produced. As we shall see in later chapters, the changing conditions of naval warfare altered the future of the battleship brand itself. Yet within a certain spectrum of design objectives, principally those of producing fast, heavily armed warships, the dreadnoughts and super-dreadnoughts had been a success.

Turbine Power

The dreadnoughts and super-dreadnoughts were mechanically powerful ships—of that there can be no doubt. By way of comparison, many modern destroyers average around 500 feet in length, have a displacement of some 8,000 tons and typically powered by an array of gas turbines, can make speeds of around 30 knots quite comfortably. Back in 1915, the British launched HMS *Royal Sovereign*, which measured 624 feet and had a fully laden displacement of 31,000 tons. Nevertheless, such a hulking ship could still make 23 knots, driven by its Parsons steam turbines and fuelled by boilers that generated 40,000shp. Such figures remain respectable even more than 100 years later.

In Profile:
Parsons Turbines

The Parsons name is a good hook on which to hang our initial discussion of the dreadnought powerplants, as it was a name that dominated British naval propulsion for crucial decades in its history. Charles Parsons was a British engineer who, during the 1880s, began experimenting with turbine powerplant systems in marine contexts, as replacements for reciprocating engines. In summary, turbines work by delivering the thermal energy of pressurized steam to blades on a rotary shaft, the steam pressure turning the shaft to provide rotary output power. Parsons built upon previous early work in turbine technology and sought to improve the efficiency of the engine type. How he did so is explained in a lecture paper he wrote in about 1904:

> In 1884 or four years previously, I dealt with the turbine problem in a different way. It seemed to me that moderate surface velocities and speeds of rotation were essential if the turbine motor was to receive general acceptance as a prime mover. I therefore decided to split up the fall in pressure of the steam into small fractional expansions over a large number of turbines in series, so that the velocity of the steam nowhere should be great. Consequently, as we shall see later, a moderate speed of turbine suffices for the highest economy. This principle of compounding turbines in series is now universally used in all except very small engines, where economy in steam is of secondary importance. The arrangement of small falls in pressure at each turbine also appeared to me to be surer to give a high efficiency, because the steam flowed practically in a non-expansive manner through each individual turbine, and consequently in an analogous way to water in hydraulic turbines whose high efficiency at that date had been proved by accurate tests.
>
> Parsons, "The Steam Turbine," c. 1904

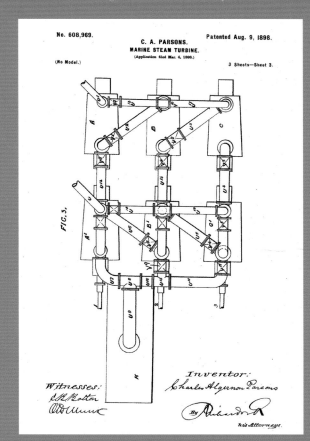

Parsons was soon proving the success of his design. The first turbine-powered ship in history, the *Turbinia*, was launched in 1894 and was given motion by a three-stage axial-flow direct-acting (i.e. not geared) Parsons steam turbine, which made the 104-feet craft for a time the fastest ship on the waves, although the ship did experience some issues with cavitation (explained and discussed below). Further military commissions followed, with Parsons turbines fitted to two navy destroyers—HMS *Viper* and HMS *Cobra*—at the turn of the 20th century. Parsons' momentum was building, and it was in 1906 that three great ships took to the waves all powered by Parsons turbines—the legendary civil liners *Lusitania* and *Mauretania*, and the battleship *Dreadnought*.

This diagram is from Parsons' patent application of 1898 for his steam turbines. The Parsons steam turbine would be the heart of almost all the dreadnought and super-dreadnought battleships.

The *Journal of the American Society for Naval Engineers* article also makes note of ash ejectors, a critical mechanical feature in any coal-powered ship. Each boiler room featured its own ash ejector, which consisted of a discharge pipe rising up from the stokehold to an ejection port set up the side of the hull. The ashes were pushed into a hopper that fed them through a grate into the discharge pipe, and the ashes were ejected by a blast of water at 200lb/sq in pressure from the boiler rooms' fire and bilge pumps. An alternative method was an ash hoist (actually little more than a bucket lift) for carrying loose ash up to the upper deck, but this was largely an emergency measure only, for it resulted in polluting ash blowing around the deck areas. Note that with the introduction of purely oil-fired ships, out went the associated need for ash ejectors.

Dreadnought had many other pump systems fitted, including four 75-ton fire and bilge pumps in the engine rooms. There were also electric pumps placed in the watertight compartments, these able to pump out 50 tons of water each hour should the crew need to evacuate a flooded compartment with haste.

Regarding the coal bunkers, these were filled via fixed coaling chutes that ran between the upper and main decks. This configuration was an improvement over earlier practices, in which coal was transferred via canvas chutes, a process that usually ended up with a filthy ship. The coal bunkers were set amidships, with each boiler having its own set of dedicated bunkers. To ensure a watertight separation between the bunker and the boiler, the bulkheads were solid with no penetration by communication systems, although some of the bunkers had watertight doors fitted.

Before looking at other aspects of *Dreadnought's* engineering arrangements, we should note the steady increase in turbine power across the dreadnoughts and super-dreadnoughts which took place as the technology was refined and improved. Hence while *Dreadnought* generated 23,000shp, the *Royal Sovereign* class nearly doubled that figure, to 40,000shp.

A Babcock & Wilcox boiler. The furnace would be built beneath the bank of water tubes, and the large tank at the top is the steam and water drum. The U-bend pipe in the middle is the superheater.

In Profile:
Main Power Arrangements of the Dreadnoughts and Super-Dreadnoughts

Ship/Class	Powerplant	Boilers	Shp
Dreadnought	Parsons direct-drive turbines driving four propellers	18 × Babcock & Wilcox	23,000
Bellerophon	Parsons direct-drive turbines driving four propellers	18 × Babcock & Wilcox (Yarrow in *Temeraire*)	23,000
St Vincent	Parsons direct-drive turbines driving four propellers	18 × Babcock & Wilcox (Yarrow in *Collingwood*)	24,500
Neptune	Parsons direct-drive turbines driving four propellers	18 × Yarrow	25,000
Colossus	Parsons direct-drive turbines driving four propellers	18 × Babcock & Wilcox (Yarrow in *Hercules*)	25,000
Agincourt	Parsons direct-drive turbines driving four propellers	22 × Babcock & Wilcox	34,000
Orion	Parsons direct-drive turbines driving four propellers	18 × Yarrow (Babcock & Wilcox in *Monarch*)	27,000
King George V	Parsons direct-drive turbines driving four propellers	18 × Babcock & Wilcox (Yarrow in *Audacious* and *Centurion*)	31,000
Iron Duke	Parsons direct-drive turbines driving four propellers	18 × Yarrow (Babcock & Wilcox in *Iron Duke* and *Benbow*)	29,000
Queen Elizabeth	Parsons reaction turbines driving four propellers	24 × Babcock & Wilcox	56,000
Royal Sovereign	Parsons reaction turbines driving four propellers	18 × Babcock & Wilcox (Yarrow in *Resolution* and *Royal Oak*)	40,000
Erin	Parsons direct-drive turbines driving four propellers	15 × Babcock & Wilcox	26,500
Canada	Parsons and Brown Curtis turbines driving four propellers	21 × Yarrow	37,000

Giving some impression of the sheer scale of battleship propulsion, here are the triple screws of the Russian *Gangut*-class dreadnought *Poltava*. The ship had 4-shaft Parsons steam turbines.

Actually the ship had four screws, not triple screws.
Note the 4-shaft turbines would have an equal number of screws.

Propellers and steering gear

The shafts from the turbines terminated in the ship's mighty three-bladed propellers, each (at the original point of design) 8 feet 10 inches in diameter and with a blade area of 33 square feet. In May/June 1907, these were all replaced, with those on the inner shafts having a reduced area of 28 square feet and the outer shaft propellers having an increased area of 40 square feet.

A key challenge of steam turbine design was that of striking the right relationship between the speed of the turbine blades, and therefore of the rotor shaft, and that of the propeller in the water. Put simply, turbines worked at their greatest efficiency at high speeds, whereas propellers required turning at lower speeds to ensure that they delivered their force with optimal "bite" on the water. This issue was addressed in dreadnought battleships through the use of a speed-reduction gear, explained here in *The Naval Annual 1913*:

> The advantage which may accrue from the introduction of speed-reduction gear between the turbine and the propeller is easily explained. Popularly expressed, the thermodynamic efficiency of a turbine depends largely on this speed of the blades around the circumference of its rotor being in proper relation to the velocity of the steam impinging on the blades. The peripheral speed of the drum of a turbine carrying the blades therefore requires [it] to be high. The screw propeller of a ship, after it exceeds a given rate of speed, falls off somewhat in efficiency owing to cavitation which, popularly explained, means the introduction of air in front of the blade surface. The result is not only a reduction in efficiency but serious deterioration of the metal by erosion. It is true that this latter difficulty has been partly overcome, but it is inevitable that with cavitation there should be great loss in the driving power of the screw. To overcome the difficulty a compromise was made by increasing the diameter of the turbine drum, so that the number of revolutions was reduced without a proportionate lessening of the blade speed, which could thus be kept not too much below the velocity of steam. At the same time the revolutions of the propeller were lessened. Increase in the diameter of the turbine rotor, however, involved considerable augmentation of weight. The difference in weight per H.P. of battleship and destroyer turbines is partly due to the latter being run at a greater number of revolutions per minute.

The Naval Annual 1913, p. 100

With the problems of cavitation solved, the dreadnought and super-dreadnought battleships could perform with control and dexterity at lower speeds, as attested to by numerous reports from the era. Of course, the ship also had to be steered, and direction was delivered through twin underhung rudders in the transverse section. (A single rudder would have given the ship an unacceptably large turning circle.) Two sets of control shafting were fitted within the ship, one set to port and one to starboard, the shafting running down to the steering engines that powered the rudders. Note, however, that each control shaft was linked to both steering engines, although a clutch system meant that only one shaft could operate a steering engine at any one time. The doubling-up was a complicated but sensible arrangement. It meant that if one control shaft were damaged by, say, a torpedo strike, the ship could still be steered via the other shaft. In the case of a dire emergency, should the standard mechanical control system break down entirely, the ship also included a manual steering compartment at the very back of the ship, in which manual brute force could be used to keep the vessel moving roughly in the right direction. All being well, however, there were actually five positions from which the ship could be steered: bridge, two positions on the conning tower, and two on the signal tower.

In Profile:

Admiralty Report: "Suggested Alterations in Ships of Dreadnought Class"

1. Efficient communication between the two starting platforms is essential. A 4-in. voice-pipe should be fitted above main deck between the engine-rooms at the maneuvering valves, and a loud single-stroke gong in lieu of the present telephonic communication. This pipe can be led above the main deck, and the thwartship bulkhead between the engine rooms kept watertight.

3. The position of the distiller test tanks should be altered, and a stowage found inside the engine-room hatches to enable the tanks to be more easily under observation, and for the better preservation of the gauge-glasses and guards. At present they are placed immediately in the gangway of two ladders from the upper to main deck.

4. Complete jointless lengths of steam pipes should be fitted in spaces between the main machinery and boiler compartments, as great difficulty has been experienced in making awkward joints in these confined spaces.

6. Arrangements for escape of air from reserve feed and oil-tanks should be made more efficient by cutting more holes in longitudinals, as at present water and oil will not level off for some hours, and filling has to take place very slowly. This is important, as a list to the ship materially increases her draft.

7. Generally it would be better not to attach oil-boxers to steam cylinders, but to fit them to bulkheads adjacent, as the oil gets very thin and hot. The dripping could be more easily regulated, and the oil would remain cooler.

11. Spring-loaded valves for escape of excess exhaust steam to auxiliary condenser should be placed in a more accessible position, since, at present, a proper adjustment of these valves is very hard to carry out.

14. A complete range of auxiliary steam pipe should be carried right around the engine and boiler rooms. The disposition of the coal is such that the forward group of boilers should be used as little as possible in harbor. With either of the other groups of boilers in use the auxiliary steam pipe forward of them has usually to be kept under steam, and the fact of there being little or no circulation of steam through this end of the pipe causes water to accumulate which finds its way out through joints and expansion glands.

17. The ice machine and refrigerator engine should both be fitted with weeds traps and also the ice machine with a non-return valve close to the sea inlet, as both these engines have been frequently choked with jelly fish, and the process of clearing occupies considerable time. The ice machine be situated on the upper deck, considerable difficulties experienced on starting machine in getting the circulating pump to heave.

24. The crush shaft between the two steering engines should be made in three pieces instead of two. There should be a flanged coupling in the port engine-room as well as in the starboard, and a short middle piece of shaft, some 6 feet in length. The present long piece cannot be removed clear of the steering engine. The plummer block for port center shaft and the steering engine cross shaft being removed.

A warship air intake cowl and weather flap, giving an air velocity in the shaft of 30ft/sec to the rooms below decks.

Electrical Systems

Dreadnought and its kin were huge physical entities, requiring prodigious amounts of electrical power to sustain their numerous functions. Principal electrical generation was provided by four Siemens dynamos, two of them driven by Brotherhood steam piston engines and two by Mirrlees diesel engines (although one of the diesel engines was replaced by a steam engine prior to commissioning, following reliability issues). These engines and dynamos could be run when the ship was not under power, such as when in harbor, and generate a total power output of 410kW, according to John Roberts' *The Battleship Dreadnought*, "supplying current at 1,000 amps and connected in parallel to a Cowan switchboard from which the 100-volt circuits were distributed on a branch system" (Roberts, p. 27). The dynamos were thunderous pieces of equipment, the steam-powered version weighing a total of 8.5 tons, while the larger diesel-powered unit weighed 17 tons. Both ran at 400rpm.

The dreadnoughts and super-dreadnoughts became increasingly hungry in terms of electrical consumption, resulting in a steady increase in generating capacity. For example, while the *Dreadnought* had a total output of 400kW, the later *Queen Elizabeth* could produce 700kW, by virtue of two 200kW turbogenerators and two 150kW diesels at 220 volts DC. By the time we get to the *King George V* class of super-dreadnought, we see each ship fitted with no fewer than eight 300kW generators (six turbo and two diesel), together delivering a total of 2,400kW of power. A key point to note in the development of dreadnought electrical power is that in 1905 the 200-volt ring main system was introduced into warship design. *Dreadnought* was intended as a beneficiary of this design, but as it happened the adoption did not take place until the *Bellerophon*-class vessels.

The central engine room of the *Iron Duke*-class dreadnought *Emperor of India*. The warship was fitted with four Parsons steam turbines, generating 29,000shp.

Dreadnought also had an extensive 15-volt DC low-power system fitted throughout the ship. Dreadnought's life, and indeed that of any battleship of this era, depended upon the delivery of electrical power, once hand power and steam-driven mechanical power began to recede into the past. Electrical power had to be applied to all manner of purposes—refrigeration, lighting, hoists lifting everything from shells to boats, the telephone communications, wireless transmissions, pumps and compressors, heating, powered workshop tools, and much more. In fact, a large dreadnought-type vessel might have in the region of 400 electrical drive motors dotted around above and below decks.

Construction of the turbines for HMS Bellerophon at the Fairfield Shipbuilding & Engineering Company in Govan, Scotland.

Some elements of Dreadnought's electrical systems were more important than others. Navigational compasses were one of them. By December 1906, Dreadnought had been fitted with three compasses, located on the bridge, compass platform, and the quarterdeck. Three types of compasses were fitted: standard, liquid, and a Siemens electrical, the first two being basic naval compasses but the latter being the only example of its type fitted to a Royal Navy warship. The electric compass was designed to provide better integration with the ship's fire-control systems, but in practice it did not perform well, so from 1911 it was replaced by a variety of gyrocompasses.

The other two compasses provided satisfactory service, although the Experimental Cruise threw up a few problems. With the standard compass, there was some deviation caused by the electromechanical interference of the ship's own magnetic character, but adjustments made at Trinidad appeared to solve the most serious of the problems. Regarding the Pattern 23 liquid compass, the main problems for this instrument came from the blast of gunfire, which shattered the plate glass on the binnacle helmet, and from the vibrations of the ship under way. The Experimental Cruise report noted:

> It is suggested that the method of suspension is not strong enough to support a compass of such weight when subjected to excessive vibration, and that a more efficient one would be to support the outer gimbal ring by stout spiral springs, on the same principle as the Kelvin's pontoon compass.

> R. C. Bacon, *Report on the Experimental Cruise*, p. 31

For communications, *Dreadnought* had a variety of internal and inter-ship systems fitted during its lifetime. The critical engineer and operational spaces were linked by a central telephone exchange located on the lower deck, through which could flow a total of 46 connections and three extensions. There were also direct connection navy phones making important individual auditory links between, for example, fire-control positions and between machinery compartments. John Roberts notes that while in the *Dreadnought* exchange lamps and call bells were powered by a motor-generator, the speaking circuits were powered by batteries (Roberts, p. 33), and in later dreadnoughts all parts of the system were generator-powered.

Looking to the battleship's wireless systems, its first fitment was the venerable Tune C Mk II set, which had an inter-ship transmission range of between 250 and 500 miles. An improved version (the Type 1) was introduced in 1911, plus a low-power, short-range Type 3 (also known as the Short Distance Set), which was intended as a replacement for flag signaling. In 1917, the wireless configuration was updated with the addition of the Type 16 auxiliary set and Type 13 after-action set, then the following year with the Type 31 fire-control set. Across the spectrum of such devices, *Dreadnought* and similar vessels had reasonable wireless communication across distances of a few hundred meters up to hundreds of miles, although visual means (flags, signal lamps, etc.) remained common at short ranges.

Ventilation and Cooling

The topic of ventilation and cooling was a critical one in warship design during the first half of the 20th century. It could be one of those intensely practical aspects overlooked or under-appreciated at the initial design stages. For those who had to live with the reality of poorly ventilated spaces, however, the designer's lack of investment could result in truly dreadful living conditions. Following the Experimental Cruise, the following observations were made about the ship's ventilation issues:

Here we see two fan blades used in battleship ventilation systems, giving a striking impression of their size. Effective ducted ventilation was critical to removing the build-up of harmful below-deck gases.

1. The following places are not ventilated, and require a supply of air:–

    Lower conning tower.

    Lower signal tower.

    Lamp-room.

    Chief of staff's office.

    Electric store and acid room.

    W.R. officers' smoking-room.

2. The following spaces are inadequately ventilated:–

    Mess decks.

    Electricians' and armourers' workshop.

    Engineers' store-room.

    Switchboard-room. (An improved trunk would rectify this.)

3. To improve the ventilation of the main deck larger fans (say 20-in.) and larger trunks should be fitted, and if possible, the trunks should be led with less bends, and the necessary bends made more gradual. Most of the air in the supply is wasted through the first few louvres and branches. These should be made smaller than the more remote ones.

4. The 12½-in. propeller fans used as exhaust fans for the seaman's head are not really necessary.

R. C. Bacon, Report on the Experimental Cruise

Two types of steam turbine-gear-driven warship fan, designed in 1918/19. For safety in case of flooding, warship bulkheads had to be unpierced, therefore fan units were the only effective means of ventilation in most below-deck areas.

Reading between the lines here, we can see how important ventilation was to maintaining the efficiency of the ship and the health of its personnel. In the list of affected spaces in points 1 and 2, we see several workshop and storage spaces that, with absent or poor ventilation, could become thick with toxic gases, or at least with overwhelming heat. Furthermore, a lack of ventilation was also a mechanical issue—an absence of moving fresh air would result in the build-up of corrosive condensation on sensitive electrical parts. Even more problematic could be the issue that excessive build-up of heat could result in machinery, such as generators and dynamos, overheating and breaking down.

These mechanical issues became even more profound when considering the sheer importance of keeping the boiler rooms fed with fresh air, both to improve the efficiency of the engines and keep the formidable heat of the spaces under control. Two editions and two reprints of the volume *The Air Supply to Boiler Rooms of Modern Ships of War* were published between 1916 and the 1921, exploring in detail the physical challenges of delivering air to boilers. The author of the 1921 edition, Richard W. Allen, makes the point that boiler ventilation, particularly on oil-fired ships, was a fundamental consideration for ship performance:

It is a well-known fact that in burning oil fuel, higher air pressures are required than for coal, and consequently the power absorbed by the fans is considerable. Any improvement which can be affected by increasing the efficiency of the system, with a consequent saving in steam consumption, reduction in weight and space occupied, will have some influence on the speed and economy of the ship.

Allen, Air Supply to Boiler Rooms, p. 3

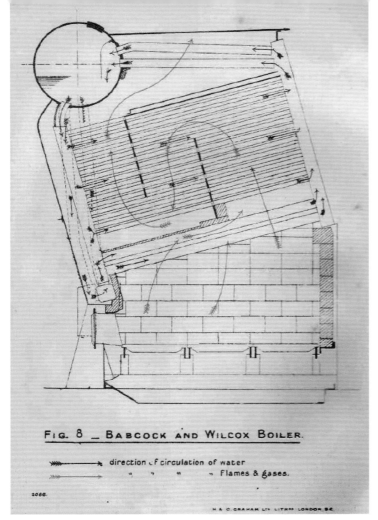

FIG. 8 _ BABCOCK AND WILCOX BOILER.

⟶⟶⟶ direction of circulation of water
⟶⟶⟶ " " " " Flames & gases.

2068.

H. & C. GRAHAM Lᵗᵈ LITHᵒ LONDON S.E.

Two diagrams explaining the function of the Babcock & Wilcox boiler, taken from *The Stoker's Manual* of 1912.

Another image from *The Stoker's Manual* of 1912, this time explaining the principles of on-board refrigeration, which was crucial to ensuring the longevity of food supplies.

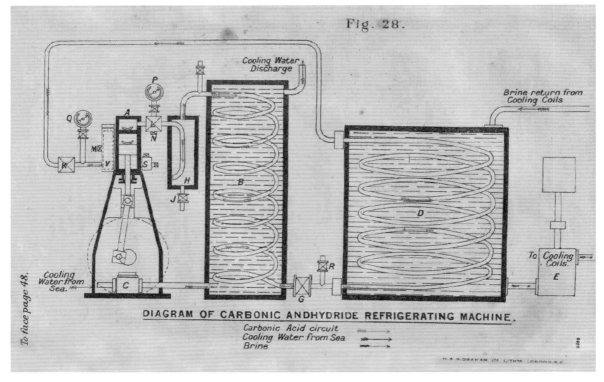

Fig. 28.

Cooling Water Discharge

Brine return from Cooling Coils

To Cooling Coils.

Cooling Water from Sea.

To face page 48.

DIAGRAM OF CARBONIC ANDHYDRIDE REFRIGERATING MACHINE.

Carbonic Acid circuit ⟶
Cooling Water from Sea ⟶
Brine ⟶

H. & C. GRAHAM Lᵗᵈ LITHᵒ LONDON S.E.

A view down the starboard side of the Brazilian battleship *Minas Geraes*, showing crew maintaining the ship's launches. From this position we are looking down on one of the twin 12-inch gun turrets.

The author also notes in passing an academic factor that was a partial explanation of the problems reported on the capital ships:

> When passing in review the difficulty of guiding the air into the entrances and through the down takes, with the least possible resistance, as well as the question of the distribution of air in the stokeholds, one is forced to the conclusion that only the fringe of this important subject has been touched, especially having regard to the growth of the naval units during the last four years, and the great increase in the power of their propelling machinery, calling for much larger quantities of air to be delivered to the fans.

Allen, Air Supply to Boiler Rooms, p. 5

Dreadnought's most visible ventilation ducts clung to the sides of the two funnels, each running down to a fan chamber supplying the boiler rooms. Below decks, the ship's ventilation was delivered through similar supply trunks fitted with electric fans, plus the usual variety of apertures that could be opened to allow the passage of fresh air. Regarding the trunks, the desirable air speed flowing through was 20–25ft/sec, although in some instances up to 48ft/sec might be desirable when heavier airflow was required. The key to effective trunking design was to provide an unimpeded airflow through the intake, then to channel that airflow through to the required space without slowing it down through too many sharp corners and obstructions.

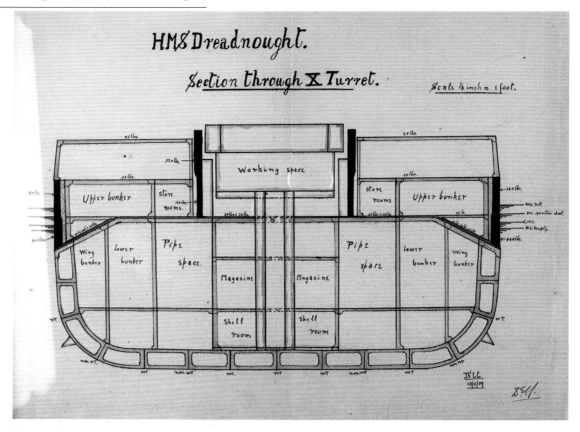

This useful cross-section diagram shows the arrangement of shell rooms and magazines around the ammunition hoist trunking, feeding up the turret working space.

A hand-tinted postcard entitled "Broadside Salvoes" depicts an early dreadnought warship delivering full broadside firepower. As in the age of sail, the broadside was the most desirable presentation of the guns to achieve fire superiority.

Turret and Barbette

There is frequently confusion over the distinction between turrets and barbettes. The confusion has arisen because in many ways the separation between the two ceased to be watertight, at least in appearance. Essentially a barbette consists of a fixed protective armored ring, in which the gun sits and rotates. A turret, by contrast, is a fully armored housing that rotates in its entirety with the gun. The advantage of the barbette is that the machinery required to move the gun does not have to be as powerful as that of a turret. However, barbettes often do not offer the high degree of protection afforded by a turret. In the late 19th century, however, barbette designs were improved with the addition of an enclosing armored gun house that rotated with the guns. These types of structures also became known as turrets. Strictly speaking, *Dreadnought* was fitted with barbettes, but turret is used as a more familiar term.

barrels meant increased velocities and therefore improved range, penetration, and weight of shot, which were deciding factors in an age of iron-clad enemies. A seminal advance came with the French invention, around 1845, of the interrupted screw system, which enabled a rapid means of loading plus, when combined with an appropriate chamber thickness, a secure means of locking against the massive pressures of detonation. The interrupted screw became one of the principal (although not the only) mechanisms for heavy guns, while sliding breechblocks were more common on lighter weapons, especially those that utilized that other major advance of the 19th century—the unitary metallic-cased shell.

Of course, it was one matter to load and fire a gun, but it was another altogether to move that gun smoothly and quickly onto the correct bearing and elevation. Yet the technologies of gun mount had also seen major progress by the time that *Dreadnought* was laid down. Hydraulic power, invented at the very end of the 18th century initially for its applications to factory machinery, made its way into naval gun machinery by the second half of the 19th century, providing a smooth, quiet, and reliable system for training the guns. The hydraulic medium was either fresh water (in some systems salt water could be drawn in if there was a sudden critical loss of hydraulic fluid) or oil; water was the preferred fluid used in British guns. Hydraulic systems were also better suited to the rapid back-and-forth training movements required in battle and were especially more resilient under the repeated changes of direction fed from mechanized fire-control systems—a true revolution in naval gunnery.

Then there was the matter of protection for the gun crews. While secondary armaments might be exposed deck guns, the main guns and their operators were too important to leave unprotected. This was where turrets and barbettes had their role. (The differences between the two are explored in the feature box "Turret and Barbette" below.) From the mid-19th century, guns were increasingly emplaced in turrets/barbettes mounted either on the deck or set into the hull structure. From the 1870s twin-gun turrets also became more common.

The combination of hydraulically powered turrets, barbettes, and mounts, plus the constant improvements in breech-loading gun technology and in the shells themselves, led to the mighty firepower of the dreadnoughts and super-dreadnoughts, guns that shook the foundations of global politics as much as they rippled the surface of the oceans.

12in Main Guns and Mounts

The main gun that graced the decks of the *Dreadnought* plus the *Bellerophon* class (also the preceding *Lord Nelson* class of pre-dreadnought and the contemporary *Invincible* and *Indefatigable* classes of battlecruiser) was the BL (breech-loading) 12in Mk X 45-cal. With a total length of 557.5 inches and weighing 56 tons, this was a substantial piece of weaponry. The breech was of the Wellin interrupted screw type, and the barrel was of a wire-wound construction, meaning that layers of steel ribbon wire were wrapped around the inner liner

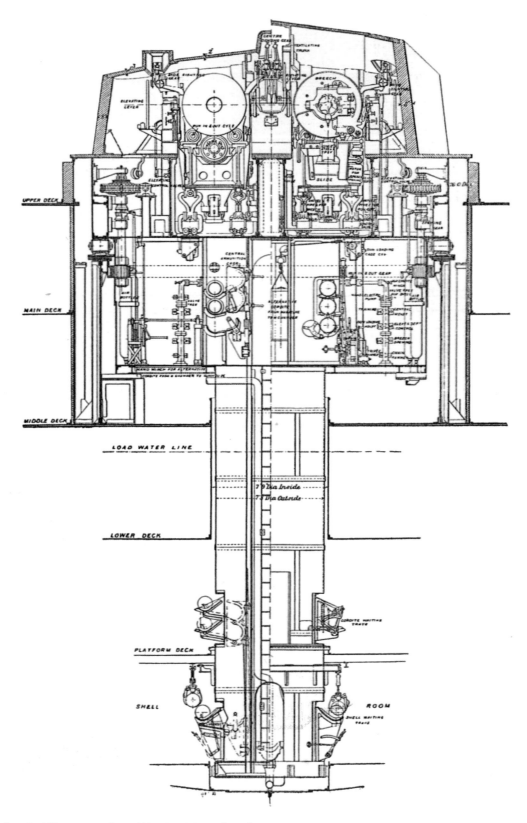

A detailed illustration from *Warships Today* (1936) shows the gunhouse and mounting for the twin 12-inch guns as mounted in *Agincourt*.

HMAS *Agamemnon*, a *Lord Nelson*-class pre-dreadnought, undergoes the replacement of one of its 12-inch guns in Malta in May/June 1915.

(which formed the bore and held the rifling), with each layer of wire having a different tension. The wire-wound gun was the preferred method of construction by many naval weapon builders at this time, as it gave a great tangential strength to the gun barrel. Some nations, especially the United States, preferred the "built-up method," made up from composite layers of forged steel, the Americans being of the opinion that this method's longitudinal strength meant avoiding the barrel droop sometimes experienced by well-worn wire-wound guns. The Mk X had a polygroove rifling system at a rate of one turn in every 30 calibers. Firing an 850lb shell propelled by 258lb bags of MD cordite, the gun could generate muzzle velocities of around 2,800ft/sec, giving a maximum range of 16,400 yards.

A view from the focsle of HMS *Renown* of its 15-inch, seen here during the World War II era when such heavy firepower proved more useful for delivering offshore naval gunfire support than engaging in ship-vs-ship duels.

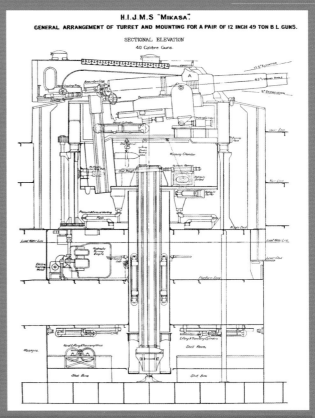

A diagram of the Elswick Ordnance Company 12-inch guns and machinery for the Japanese battleship *Mikasa*, the illustration suggesting the journey of a shell from shell room to gun breech.

In Profile:
Shell-loading Procedure

Across the dreadnoughts and super-dreadnoughts, there were numerous different mechanical arrangements for transferring shells and cordite bags to the ship's main guns. However, there were some general principles of operation. The 12-inch shells were stored deep down in the ship, below the waterline, in shell rooms, with the corresponding propellant bags being held in the nearby magazines, usually located above the shell rooms. The shell rooms, magazines and handling rooms (spaces for preparing the propellant for delivery to the turret) would be positioned around a central ammunition lift, which contained hoists and unitary (typical in British designs) or separate cages for lifting the ammunition components straight up to the turret directly above. One hoist or set of hoists would serve each gun. A "working chamber" sat directly beneath the rotating turret structure—note that the working chamber plus the lifting trunk all rotate in sympathy with the turret, to ensure alignment of the hoists with the guns. Also note that flashproof doors and scuttles were fitted into the trunk and other positions along the path of ammunition travel, these closing after the passage of ammunition to ensure that there was no direct passage for flame to move between the deck/turret and the magazines, should the upper parts of the ship be hit by enemy shellfire. The occupants of the working chamber could also communicate, via voice pipe, directly with the personnel in the shell rooms and handling rooms below. From the handling rooms, shells and propellant bags would be placed into the hoist cages (the heavy shells were lifted by a hydraulic grab) and raised to the working chamber, which also held some ready ammunition in case the hydraulics for the trunk failed for some reason. When the guns were ready to fire, the ammunition would be lifted via a gun-loading cage to the turret, where each component was aligned with the breech and loaded into place by telescopic rammers. The breech could now be closed, and the gun fired.

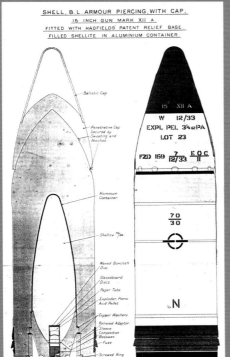

This cross-section diagram of a 15-inch naval shell illustrates the limited space for explosive filling plus the location of the base inertia fuse.

This hand-tinted postcard reads, "Big Guns and Officers and Crew of HMS *Queen Elizabeth*." A ship's cat is being reluctantly inserted into one of the eight giant 15-inch guns.

ranges, furthermore, the main guns would have a limited utility.) For this reason, the ship was heavily fitted with searchlight systems, which were tactically and practically integrated into the fire control. The previously quoted naval document explains the configuration of these searchlights:

> Twelve 36-in. searchlight projectors are mounted. Each of these is allotted an arc of 30°, and all 12 lights are controlled from the top of the fore chart-house, where they are under the captain's immediate supervision. Alternative positions for controlling them are on the main control position and after signal tower for the foremost and after lights respectively.
>
> Four of the searchlights (Ns. 2 and 5 each side) have their training and elevation electrically controlled by means of levers on top of fore chart-house and can also be switched on or off from there. The remaining eight are elevated and trained by hand at the searchlight itself, the following signals being made from the top of the fore chart-house:–
>
> | | |
> |---|---|
> | "Burn" | "Train right" |
> | "Elevate" | "Train left" |
> | "Depress | "Sweep" |
>
> These orders being conveyed by electric lamps, which can be lit or extinguished by means of switches on top of the fore chart-house.

In 1903, development began in earnest to produce a new 4-inch high-velocity gun, to give a boost to British warship secondary armament. The output of this development entered service with the *Bellerophon* class of dreadnoughts as the 4in BL Mk VII and 4-inch guns would feature on dreadnoughts and super-dreadnoughts until the 60-inch guns took over in the *Iron Duke* class. Set either on the deck or in hull sponsons, the guns measured 208.45 inches long and could throw out 4-inch shells at a muzzle velocity of 2,864ft/sec. The rate of fire was around 6–8rpm, and with an elevation of 15° the range was 11,600 yards. Note that the maximum

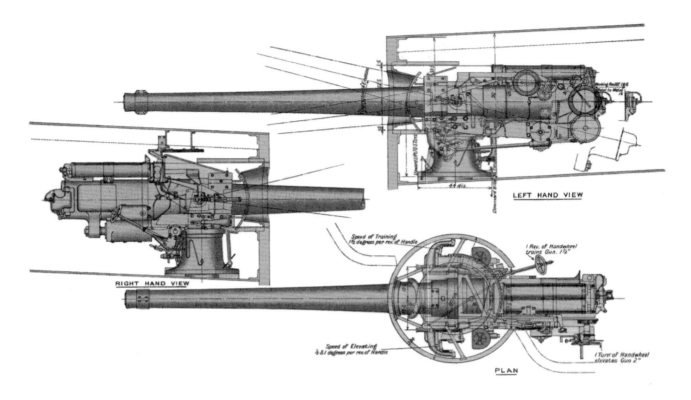

An Ordnance BL 6-inch 45-caliber gun, on a P.IX mounting. This diagram shows details of the elevator and training gears.

elevation of most of mounts for the Mk VII (specifically the P.II, P.II*, P.IV*, P.IV**, P.VI, and P.VIII) was 15°, but some guns were also set on HA (high-altitude) anti-aircraft mountings that had a maximum elevation of 60°. The guns were manually trained and fired by percussion or electrical ignition.

What the 6-inch guns offered was a far greater impact on target and a much-improved range capability, meaning that the battleship (or other vessel—the 6-inch guns were popular on a variety of ships) could engage torpedo boats at beyond-torpedo range. The Mk VII had a maximum range of 17,870 yards at 20° elevation, although 15° was more typical of the maximum elevation of most of the mounts. Muzzle velocity from the 269.5-inch bore was 2,536ft/sec, while at 2,500 yards the armor-piercing capped (APC) shells were capable of penetrating a single caliber of Krupp armor.

The downside of the 6-inch guns was that the heavy shells—each weighing around 100lb—resulted in slower rates of fire. Hoists were needed to supply the shells from the shell rooms, and during combat conditions it was recognized that these often couldn't keep the guns fed quickly enough to sustain their theoretical rate of fire of 5–7rpm. This rate could be achieved momentarily while the gunners were using up their ready ammunition, but once this was depleted the rate could drop down to just 3rpm.

The 6-inch gun type essentially questioned the all-big-gun philosophy, but it remained the preferred secondary armament for the rest of the super-dreadnought types. Other guns that could be found aboard dreadnoughts and super-dreadnoughts were small deck-mounted saluting and/or signaling guns, plus 3-inch anti-aircraft guns, to deal with the nascent threat from maritime air power.

In Profile:
Shells and Propellant

While the secondary armament on Britain's battleships typically had unitary shell and case designs, for the main guns the propellant and shells were stored and loaded as separate entities. The propellant favored by the Royal Navy was known as Cordite MD, this being adopted at the turn of the 20th century as an improved version of the Cordite Mk I. Compared to its predecessor, the Cordite MD (composition: 65 percent guncotton, 30 percent nitroglycerine, 5 percent petroleum jelly) was more stable than Cordite Mk I, and actually required 15 percent more weight to deliver the same muzzle velocity. It was, however, far less corrosive than the Mk I formula, essentially doubling the life of the barrel. The cordite was stored in quarter-charge silk bags, packed in behind the shell according the amount of power required. When the propellant was detonated, the bag was instantly burned away.

Three of HMAS *Australia*'s 12-inch gun shells on display at the Royal Australian Navy's museum at Garden Island in Sydney. The shell on the left is the Mk XA capped armor-piercing shell, while that on the right is a Mk 6A capped common-pointed shell. A shrapnel shell is in the center. (Nick Dowling)

In terms of the shells used, by the dreadnought era armor penetration was imperative, so the most common shells for naval battle were armor-piercing varieties. The most basic of these was the standing armor-piercing (AP) shell, containing only 3–5 percent high-explosive filling, detonated by an inertia-activated fuse set in the base of the shell. With its forged steel, heat-hardened body, the AP shell was designed to penetrate deep into an enemy warship's structure before the rapid deceleration triggered the fuse. However, with increased depths and improved thicknesses of armor came the need for greater penetrative abilities. This gave rise to APC shells. With these shells, the nose was fitted with a steel cap that served to weaken the impact area before the hardened steel nose of the shell could affect its penetration. In contrast, however, there were also semi-armor-piercing (SAP) warheads, which had deliberately reduced penetration so that could be fired at softer-skinned smaller warships, without the shell passing straight through before detonation.

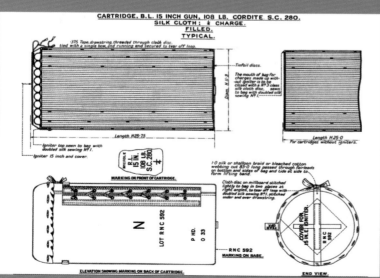

A diagram of the British Cordite S.C. 280 cartridge, here showing a quarter charge that weighed 108lb. Such charges were stacked into the breech of the BL 15-inch Mk I naval gun.

A 41cm (16in) 45-caliber 3rd Year Type naval gun from the Japanese *Nagato*-class dreadnought battleship *Mutsu*, on display outside the Yamato Museum in October 2008. The breech was of the Wellin interrupted screw type, with a single-motion screw that enabled fast reloading.

Torpedo Tubes

The dreadnoughts and the super-dreadnoughts carried two to four submerged torpedo tubes, initially of 18-inch diameter rising later to 21-inch. The pay-off for the investment in torpedo technology on these huge ships is questionable—they were fired very infrequently in battle, and in some cases, spaces devoted to torpedo storage were eventually turned over to far more desirable magazines for high-angle (HA) ammunition. The problems associated with torpedo tubes and their ammunition spaces were, specifically, the additional risk of transporting the high-explosive content and, second, the more serious risk of flooding in the spaces needed to operate torpedoes.

The torpedo tubes themselves were of a new Type B, which had a redesigned "chopper" rear door that, when combined with the side door, made the side-loading of the torpedoes more convenient. It should be noted, however, that the ingress of water through the torpedo tubes during emergency loading could result in the torpedo-room operators sloshing around in several feet of water.

The Italian crew of the *Conte di Cavour* roll a 45cm (17.7in) torpedo out ready for loading into the submerged tube, the rear of which is visible on the left of the picture.

Fire Control

Accurate, controllable, and responsive fire control was one of the fundamental challenges of the era of the big gun. The computations that had to be fed into the gunlaying process were multiple and complex—the range and bearing of the enemy, and his predicted maneuvers before gun firing and during shell flight; the movement of the firing ship relative to the enemy ship; the pitch and roll of the ship in the sea; the arcing trajectory of the shell; the ballistic conditions prevailing; the condition of the gun and the type of ammunition used—the list went on.

Technical and tactical improvements in fire control—the method of delivering shells accurately on target—had been in development since the end of the 19th century. Aided by the more rapid training capabilities of hydraulically powered mounts, gunners began using a "continuous aim" principle—actually keeping their guns on target throughout ship movement, rather than waiting with fixed barrels for a particular point in the roll to fire. This was a procedural improvement, but the real empowerment of the long-range big gun came from technology.

First came the rangefinder, which emerged functionally in the 1890s. *Dreadnought* was fitted with two Barr & Stroud 9-feet rangefinders, located on the foretop and a platform from the signal tower. Basically, the rangefinder consisted of two lenses or mirrors separated by a fixed distance (9 feet in the case of *Dreadnought*'s devices). Viewing an enemy ship produced a split image through the viewfinder, which could be used to calculate the ship's range through triangulation as the two parts of the image were adjusted to correspond. In

A collection of Barr & Stroud range-finding instruments, including a particularly large coincidence rangefinder at top, as seen in a 1936 edition of *Warships Today*.

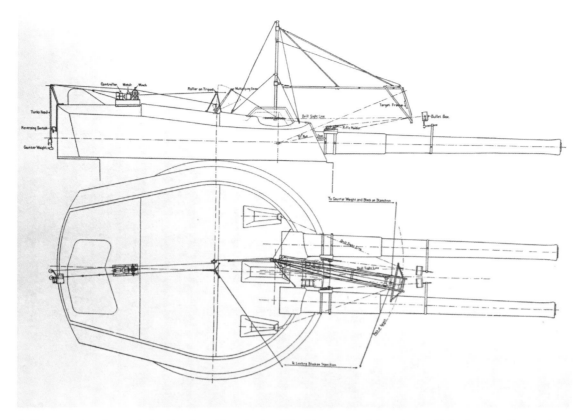

A diagram showing a deflection teaching device fitted to a pair of Armstrong 14-inch guns; the device was used to train gunners and fire-control officers how to calculate the right amount of lead to make the shell intersect with a moving target.

A BL 4-inch gun Mk VII gun from the *Indefatigable*-class battlecruiser HMS *New Zealand*, the weapon standing today in front of Auckland Museum. The warship had 16 of these anti-torpedo-boat guns. (Nick-D)

The Brazilian dreadnought *Minas Geraes* photographed from the bow. Until modernization in the United States in the 1920s, the warship did not have modern rangefinders and fire-control instruments.

The U.S. battleship USS *South Carolina* (BB-26). With 12-inch main guns, *Carolina*'s secondary battery consisted of 22 × 3in/50 guns mounted in casemates along the side of the hull.

countered with assertions that rapid fire from substantial secondary guns would provide destructive saturation of a target that the big guns would struggle to match.

The full intricacies of this argument are explored in exhaustive detail in other volumes. By way of illustration, however, we do well to examine a dreadnought defense from a "Paper Prepared by the Director of Naval Ordnance—*Considerations of the Design of a Battleship*." What is particularly interesting about this account—part of which is reproduced here—is that the author takes on the esteemed American naval strategist Alfred Thayer Mahan, author of the landmark work, *The Influence of Sea Power Upon History, 1660–1783* (1890). In the following passage, the author centrally addresses the comparison of the big guns with smaller calibers:

> It is undoubtedly true that gun of 10-inch, 9.2-inch, or 6-inch caliber will, owing to their greater rapidity of fire and the larger number that can be carried for the same weight, obtain a greater number of hits than 12-inch guns in a given time at all probable fighting range, but the increased rate of hitting with the smaller gun will be in any way proportionate to its maximum possible rate of fire as compared to that of the larger gun. Because for instance a 6-inch gun at gunlayers' test has made 11 hits in one minute it is entirely erroneous to deduce, as some writers would argue, that a broadside of five 6-inch guns would plant 55 hits per minute on an enemy. Recent experience, which is very considerable, shows that the technical requirements for attaining the highest accuracy of shooting at all ranges under battle conditions preclude entirely the effective use of more than a certain number of guns of the calibers under consideration or more than a certain rate of fire. 12-inch, 10-inch, and 9.2-inch and less calibers all come under precisely the same conditions in this respect. Therefore the inherent possibility of obtaining largely increased numbers and a much greater rate of fire from the lesser calibers cannot be realized in practice.

This disposes of the argument put forward even by so skilled a writer as Captain Mahan in the May number of the 'National Review', where he states:–

"Tactically a fleet of 'Dreadnoughts,' in action with the type hitherto in favor, requires distant firing. It therefore has received a check when an opponent can advance numerous lighter guns within effective range of its fewer heavier, which will reproduce in great measure the fight of a fleet with an embrasured fort, where large superiority in number of guns, and nearness, were essential factors to success, by beating down the personnel under a storm of light missiles, such as grape and canister. In such cases, volume of fire was relied upon to counterbalance, offensively, the great defensive inferiority of the ships' sides; and in the case of ship against ship, where so great defensive disparity will not obtain, it is well within the limits of probability that a great volume of fire may prove distinctly superior to one of less diffusion, although of equal weight."

It is improbable that Captain Mahan has ever seen fleet firing under modern conditions, or he would hardly have fallen into such error as the quotation above shows, and he would realize that the ship armed with a lighter natures of gun would be disabled long before she could close sufficiently to use them with effect even assuming her to have the advantage of speed.

Considerations of the Design of a Battleship, pp. 18–19

Although not all battle-tested authorities come to the same conclusion as in the passage above, the author does make the important distinction between theory and experience. The author argues that in the new era of the big guns, ships with lesser calibers predominating are at an automatic disadvantage, a disadvantage that would soon be exposed once 12-inch shells began to roar in, and at extreme ranges. Although this chapter has focused largely on a technical and structural description of dreadnought gunnery, we do need to remind ourselves of the psychological and physical impact of the new big-gun battleships. A full broadside of 12-inch firepower, landing in close proximity to the enemy ship or ploughing directly into its masts, decks, or other structures, must have left an impression as awe-inspiring as it was appalling. Against such firepower, any theoretical argument could be fundamentally weakened.

These dismounted BL 15-inch Mk I naval guns were originally made for HMS *Resolution* and HMS *Ramillies*. Each could fire a 1,938lb shell at a muzzle velocity of 2,640ft/sec, at ranges of more than 16 miles. (Tony Hisgett)

The crew of the Japanese Navy battlecruiser *Yamashiro* tests the ship's torpedo defense net at Yokosuka, Japan, in 1915. Torpedo nets became increasingly ineffective against new generations of torpedoes, and warship designers came to rely more upon hull torpedo bulges.

Battleship, → not battlecruiser correctly identified on P. 200.

In Profile:
Gunnery Report on Experimental Cruise

R. C. Bacon, *Report on the Experimental Cruise*

The gunnery practices were of two distinct natures:–

1) Heavy gun firing to test the best method of firing the guns so as to obtain the greatest rapidity and freedom from 'smoke interference', and also to determine the best form of control both when firing at a single ship, and also with one broadside at two ships.

2) The best grouping and control of the light Q.F. armament to repel torpedo craft by day and by night.

The details of the firings will be found in various appendices and reports attached to the gunnery and searchlight sections.

Briefly, the more important conclusions arrived at were as follows:–

1) Smoke difficulties with three-quarter charges in this climate were found to be slight. I hope to be allowed to repeat some of the firing with full charges under the climatic conditions of the English Channel, but I do not anticipate that even there any great difficulties will be found to exist.

2) The control of the guns was found to be simple, both from aloft, and from the control position on top of the signal tower.

3) The shooting gave promise and very efficient firing in action, both as regards rapidity and accuracy.

4) The type of armament was far simpler and more accurate to control than a mixed armament.

As regards the light Q.F. firing, the methods adopted were primarily governed by the consideration that the

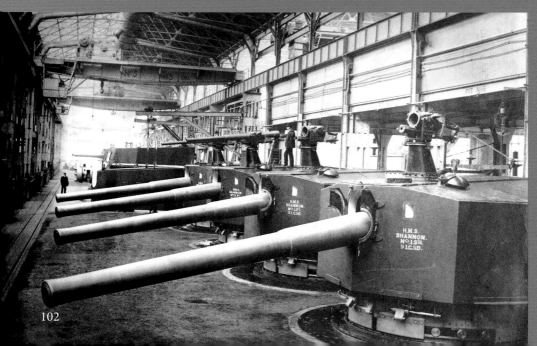

Vickers Shipbuilding & Engineering Ltd. (VSEL) in Barrow-in-Furness, Cumbria, was a major center for naval armament production, including for dreadnoughts. Here we see BL 9.2-inch Mk XI guns destined for the armored cruiser HMS *Shannon*, a Minotaur-class vessel.

A muzzle-end view of a pair of HMS *Dreadnought*'s 12-inch guns, with two QF 12-pdr 18-cwt anti-torpedo boat guns mounted on the turret roof, later to be removed.

system of control must be such as could be carried out on the night following a day action, and after the ship had been submitted to shell-fire.

I have no believer in attempting to forecast the probable success or a torpedo attack in war time from the results of firing at a canvas target at night, or by attacking ships with destroyers when only blank ammunition is fired; but night firing, if rigidly carried out, affords an excellent opportunity of judging the progress made in the defence of ships against torpedo attack.

The conclusions arrived at were:–

1) The result of the night firing was satisfactory, showing that five or six hits would probably be made by four guns on a target the size of a destroyer, or on each of the two targets the size of the destroyer, between the ranges of 2,500 and 1,500 yards.

2) The results are capable of great improvement in the near future, since many weak points our methods and practice were brought to light during the firing. I am bound to admit that this is the only night firing I have ever witnessed which in any way has led me to hope that a ship might be defended by gun-fire against a torpedo attack at night.

3) Ranging salvoes then breaking into independent firing appears to be the most satisfactory system.

4) The telaupad system of control is far and away the most efficient.

5) The control of the guns should be aloft.

6) The control of the lights should be near the captain.

7) These two controls should therefore be dissociated.

8) The arcs of training of both guns and searchlights should be unlimited.

9) Better vent-sealing tubes are required in high-pressure guns.

10) A 24-in. projector is practically as good as a 36-in.

11) The relative efficiency of two 24-in. projectors compared with one 36-in. requires further trial.

R. C. Bacon, *Report on the Experimental Cruise*, p. 5

Vice-Admiral Sir Doveton Sturdee, Flag Officer Commanding (FOC) the 4th Battle Squadron, on board the *Colossus*-class dreadnought HMS *Hercules*.

4

The Life of the Crew

"When a number of people have to live and work together, there must be rules and discipline if they are to live comfortably and to work properly. At school there is a time for everything, and punctuality is a virtue which is its own reward, though lack of it involves penalties. This school is divided one way for work, another for games, and another for eating and sleeping. That is the school routine, and routine is even more necessary on board ship" (*Wonder Book of the Navy*, p. 83). This quotation, from a title published in the 1920s, is a useful lead-in to this chapter's theme. First, the fact that the book was a children's volume did not separate it too distinctly from the concern of many serving sailors who were, after all, often in their mid- to late teens. Second, the comparison to a school is guiding. Schools, just like dreadnoughts, partly thrived on one particular quality—order, often embodied in deeply engrained routines and buttressed by an esprit de corps.

Battle was a rare event for the dreadnoughts. In this oil painting by Oswald Moser, wounded sailors are soothed by listening to musicians playing on board ship. (Science Museum Group; Wellcome Collection gallery)

Cats and dogs were naturally popular battleship mascots, but HMS *Canopus* had a goat in this role, the animal having been brought back from a voyage to the Falkland Islands.

A dramatic representation of *Dreadnought*'s searchlight piercing a gloomy northern sky.

Thurs. Sept. 16th

6.30 a.m.

Joined HMS *Dreadnought*. Shown around the ship. Went outside during the forenoon practicing for night defense. Anchored at noon. Weighed anchor 8 p.m. and proceeded to practice for night defense. The principles of night defense are to test the ability of a ship to hit another ship under the following conditions,

1) Ability to hit a single boat as soon as possible after the searchlights have been switched on. 2nd. The ability to discover another ship and engage with her <u>without</u> searchlights. 3rd. The ability to discover and engage with ships <u>with</u> searchlights. The tests were carried [out] in four ways. 1) Firing at torpedo boat target towed by another ship. 2) This is the same as (1) only other guns are brought to bear on the target. 3) Discovering and engaging with targets moored at sea without the use of searchlights. 4) This is the same as (3) only searchlights are used. In tests 1 + 2 the range can be anything between 800 [and] 12,000 yards; Tests 3 + 4 must not be less than 2,000 yards. In many cases the time limit is 2 minutes after the target has first been seen.

Frid. 17th

Proceeded to Galspia(?) bay [*sic* Golspie, Scotland] and anchored there during the forenoon. Having taken aboard umpires for night defence competition, at 8 p.m. weighed anchor and proceeded to carry out the test already stated above. Anchored at 12.30 p.m. in Dornoch(?) bay [in Scotland].

Sat. 18th

At 5 a.m. the next morning we weighed anchor and proceeded to Cromarty Firth. There was a low-lying mist all around but it did not hinder the navigation of the ship. We moored in our usual billet.

At visual ranges semaphore signaling was still used into the World War II era, although after Jutland the improvement of short-range wireless communications was recommended.

A Royal Marine sentry wakes the captain of a warship in the morning. Reversing previous trends, HMS *Dreadnought* had the officers' accommodation located forward, the theory being that the officers would be nearer to the centers of command at all times.

Sunday 19th

In the afternoon a footer match was arranged between ourselves and the *Bellerophon* and resulted in a victory for us after a hard-fought game. Sunday being wet divisions and church were held on the main deck.

Monday 20th

Several officers from the ship attended court martial held on board the *Irresistible* to try a chief petty of this ship for stealing. The case was not however proved, and the prisoner was acquitted. During the afternoon watch, it was discovered, just in time, that the beef contractor had endeavored to deposit some bags of potatoes and vegetables on the port after ladder. Fortunately, a couple of hands were quick taking the goods back in the boat again just as it was shoving off. The skipper was furious, but he did not know the flag commander was on top just waiting for a boat to come alongside. The admiral gave a dance on the quarter deck which, from all accounts, was a great success. In the afternoon a serious accident occurred to one of the midshipmen of the *King Edward VII*. He fell off the cliffs at Nigg(?) [near Cromarty Firth, Scotland] and although at present he remains alive, he has fractured his skull badly.

In the space of just four days, we see the broad spectrum of life on board *Dreadnought*, from training in gunnery practice to dealing with disciplinary issues. Such accounts are useful for reminding us that the crews of the great dreadnoughts and super-dreadnoughts spent the vast majority of their service life not in combat, but rather in the experience of the running of a great ship, an end that was worthy in itself.

"Engineer Branch"

The roles and responsibilities of the Engineer Branch would appear to speak for themselves. The personnel of this branch were tasked with keeping the ship mechanically functional, particularly in relation to the powerplant, auxiliary machinery and electrical systems.

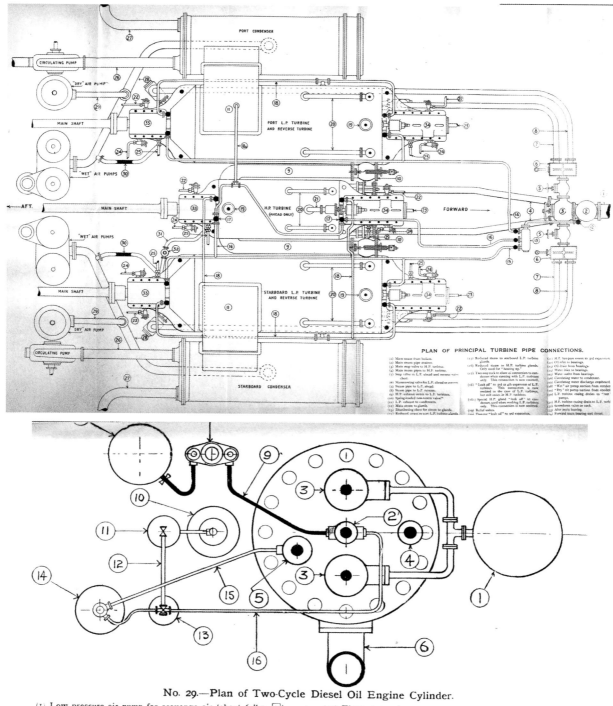

PLAN OF PRINCIPAL TURBINE PIPE CONNECTIONS.

No. 29.—Plan of Two-Cycle Diesel Oil Engine Cylinder.

(1) Low pressure air pump for scavenge air (about 6 lbs. ").
(2) Fuel valve.
(3, 3) Scavenge air valves.
(4) Safety valves (loaded to about 1200 lbs. ").
(5) Starting valve.
(6) Exhaust from exhaust belt to silencer
(7) Oil fuel tank.
(8) Fuel pump.
(9) Fuel oil pipe to fuel valve.

(10) Three-stage air compressor.
(11) After cooler.
(12) High pressure air delivery to high pressure bottle.
(13) High pressure air bottle for fuel injection purposes (800 lbs. " or more).
(14) Lower pressure air bottle for starting purposes (500 lbs. ").
(15) Starting air pipe to valve.
(16) High pressure blast air pipe to fuel valve.

Naval engineers were a technical elite amongst the warship crew, requiring a high degree of literary knowledge. Here we see technical diagrams from *Verbal notes and sketches for marine engineers* (1917).

The 1908 *Complement* lists *Dreadnought*'s engineering personnel as follows:

Engineer Commander or	
Engineer Lieutenant of over 8 years' seniority	1
Engineer Lieutenant of less than 8 years' seniority or	
Engineer Sub-Lieutenant	3
Chief Artificer Engineer or Artificer Engineer	2
Chief Engine Room Artificer	4
Engine Room Artificer	16
Chief Stoker	9
Mechanician	up to 6

A battleship has its hull paintwork refreshed. Some dreadnoughts and super-dreadnoughts were given ship camouflage color schemes, particularly angular "dazzle" camouflage.

Stoker Petty Officer	14
Leading Stoker	14
Stoker	158

The technical skill and practical knowledge embodied in these personnel was truly extensive. Naturally officers and artificers connected to the engine room were experts in all matters relating to *Dreadnought*'s powerplant and naval propulsion, but even those lower down the rankings had to wield considerable know-how. For example, and looking outside the Royal Navy documentation momentarily, the U.S. Navy's *Naval Artificer*'s manual of 1914 indirectly explains the scope of the engineer's role aboard a warship by describing the content of the manual:

King George V inspects U.S. Navy seamen at Dunkirk, France, in 1918.

Crew members of the Royal Navy *Iron Duke*-class battleship HMS *Emperor of India* recover a torpedo after a trial run. This pre-dreadnought ship was fitted with no fewer than seven 18-inch torpedo tubes.

Super

"Medical Branch"

The Medical Branch of a warship was responsible for the health, hygiene, and medical treatment of the crew. They were invariably kept busy. Even in peacetime, there would have been an endless litany of accidents and illnesses to contend with, the inevitable consequence of close life aboard a ship replete with dangerous equipment, slippery ladders, and munitions. *Dreadnought's* medical facilities would have permitted the medical team to perform all manner of surgery and disease treatment, although for very serious issues the preference was naturally for transfer to a land-based hospital as soon as possible.

The medical team would also be the center of information about general health practices. A huge problem in the navy at this time, as evidenced by contemporary naval medical reports, was venereal disease contracted during shore leave. More than 50 percent of medical issues could be related to afflictions like gonorrhea and syphilis. Other common illness such as tuberculosis, plus tropical ailments like malaria, meant the ship's medical quarters remained busy.

The Medical Branch personnel listed for *Dreadnought* in 1908 were:

Fleet of Staff Surgeon or Surgeon	1
Surgeon	2
Chief S.B. Steward	1
Second S.B. Steward	1
S.B. Attendant	1

Other Branches

An often overlooked but critical component of the ship's crew was the Accountant Branch, headed by the paymaster and assisted by a small team of assistants, clerks, and writers. This team would oversee the financial arrangements of the ship, from the crew's pay through to the purchase of food and other supplies when in port. Notably, many of the ship's cooking personnel are listed under the Accountant Branch, doubtless because their efforts depended upon sound management of the food budget and their effective use of the stores.

The cookery personnel listed for *Dreadnought* are:

Chief Ship's Cook	2
Ship's Cook	1
Leading Cook's Mate	3
Cook's Mate or 2nd Cook's Mate	4

There was also a separate branch listed as "Officers' Stewards and Cooks." Within this category, 1st, 2nd, and 3rd class stewards/cooks were assigned to the commanding officer, wardroom, gun room and warrant officers, ensuring that the upper hierarchy of the ship was well served and entertained.

RATHMULLAN PIER. LOUGH. SWILLY. Co. DONEGAL. 9301 W L

Royal Navy personnel seen at Rathmullan Pier on Lough Swilly in Co. Donegal, Ireland, August 1906, just as the dreadnought age was about to make its mark. Identified boats are HMS *Arrogant*, HMS *Majestic*, and HMS *King Edward VII*.

In Profile:
Suggested Cookery Improvements from the Experimental Cruise

Cooking Apparatus

46. More simple and more suitable arrangements for the supply of water to the boiler are necessary. As fitted in "Dreadnought" the fittings are frequently getting choked, and the greatest care and attention is necessary to prevent an accident. A large hand pump for feeding the boiler is required.

47. Two more hot chests would be a convenience. These could be fitted where the iron cupboard is now placed, the cupboard being useless owing to its proximity to the galley.

48. The floor space should be tiled. It would give a smart appearance and could be easily kept clean, whereas the present conolite quickly wears into holes and never looks clean.

Bakery

48A. It is very beneficial to have a separate compartment in which to work the dough apart from, and adjacent to, the oven, and the arrangements in "Dreadnought" are very satisfactory. The place where the dough is worked should be free from draughts and should be fitted with sashes to open and not gratings.

48B. Floor space of bakery should be tiled.

49. A clock and thermometer should form part of the establishment of every bakery.

A posed photograph of common sailors aboard the Brazilian dreadnought *Minas Geraes*. A mutiny aboard the ship on November 22, 1910, by Afro-Brazilian crew members following the lashing of one of their men, saw the captain and several other leading personnel murdered. The mutiny spread to other ships in the fleet. (George Grantham Bain Collection)

Not a dreadnought but the German pre-dreadnought *Kaiser Friedrich III*. Extensive modernizations to the ship in 1908 could still not make it relevant to the dreadnought age, and it was deactivated in late 1915.

In an image originally published in *The Illustrated War News* on January 27, 1915, we see the German armored cruiser SMS *Blücher*. Armored cruisers were steadily rendered more or less redundant by the modern battlecruiser.

The German battlecruiser SMS *Seydlitz* underway. Battlecruisers were very much part of the dreadnought revolution, often exhibiting the same "all-big-gun" philosophy but without the heavy weight of armor.

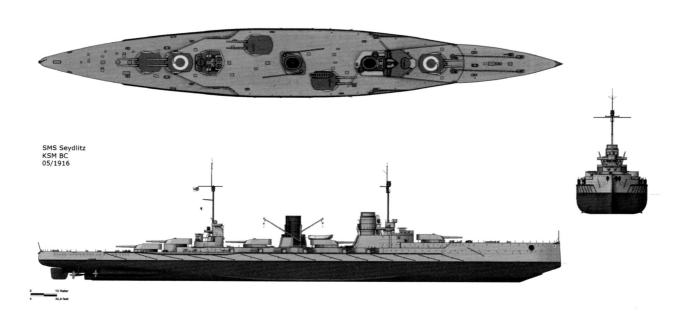

SMS Seydlitz
KSM BC
05/1916

0   10 Meter
0   32.0 feet

A digitally rendered plan of SMS *Seydlitz*, the top artwork showing the funnel and the gun arrangement. *Seydlit* had the most punishing war—at the battle of Jutland it was hit more than 20 times by enemy shells. (Alexpl)

In Profile:
Bayern

altering the balance of power in the Mediterranean. They were, however, Austria-Hungary's only dreadnoughts; plans for another class came to nothing. Yet the Austro-Hungarian shipbuilding program was sufficient to motivate the Regia Marina Italiana (Italian Navy) to lean into its own commitments to the dreadnought type.

By the turn of the 20th century, Italy had developed a giant, if a little slow, shipbuilding industry, especially through building an effective working relationship with British skills and infrastructure. From the 1880s through the first decade of the 20th century, Italian shipyards had produced no fewer than 11 ironclads and pre-dreadnought vessels. The last of these was within the *Regina Elena* class, constructed between 1901 and 1908 and comprising four ships—*Regina Elena, Vittorio Emanuele III, Roma,* and *Napoli.* The class was designed by the great Vittorio Cuniberti, a foundational figure in the history of the dreadnought and naval warfare in general (see profile following). They were fast ships, capable of attaining 22 knots (25mph) through triple-expansion steam engines and were armed with a mix of 30.5cm (12in), 20.3cm (8in), and 7.6cm (3in) guns with two 45cm (17.7in) torpedo tubes.

Italy's first true dreadnought, however, was the product of Cuniberti's all-big-gun idea and the design skills of Rear Admiral Engineer Edoardo Masdea, Chief Constructor of the Regia Marina Italiana: it was the battleship *Dante Alighieri.* True to Cuniberti's vision, the ship had a displacement of just under 20,000 tons, was powered by four steam turbines to a speed of 22 knots (25mph) and was armed with 12×30.5cm (12in) guns set in four triple turrets along the centerline (one forward, one aft, and two set amidship between the funnels). Armor depth along the waterline belt was 10 inches.

The pre-dreadnought Italian battleship *Vittorio Emanuele* in World War I. The ship had a particularly imbalanced armament, consisting of 4×30.5cm (12in) guns and 12×20.3cm (8in) guns.

In Profile:
Vittorio Cuniberti (1854–1913)

Vittorio Emilio Cuniberti was a leading visionary behind the dreadnought concept, taking ideas already bubbling away in international navies but giving them a shape and clarity that galvanized the development and launch of HMS *Dreadnought* itself. Born in Turin in 1854, Cuniberti joined the Genio Navale (Corps of Naval Engineering) in 1878, and quickly demonstrated a prodigious talent in military maritime engineering and shipbuilding. His landmark practical achievement was his design of the *Regina Elena* class of pre-dreadnoughts, but in the early years of the 20th century he also laid out a theoretical vision of the future, one that he expressed with greatest impact in an article for *Jane's All the World's Fighting Ships* in 1903, entitled "An Ideal Battleship for the British Fleet." Here Cuniberti mapped out his vision for what would become the dreadnought type, c. 17,000 tons displacement: heavily armed with a single caliber of main guns, capable of delivering a crushing big-gun broadside; driven fast by steam turbines; brutishly armored to shrug off the impacts of enemy shells. In the article, he outlined the concept clearly and ended his thoughts with a practical vision of how it might be realized:

The Italian battleship *Dante Alighieri* in Taranto, 1917. The warship participated in the second battle of Durazzo on October 2, 1918, as part of a mixed Allied force bombarding Austro-Hungarian shore defenses, and attacked the enemy-held port at Durazzo, Albania.

I would say frankly at once that the designs for such a vessel have already been worked out, and that its construction seems quite feasible and attainable. Following up the progressive scale of displacements from 8000 to 12,000, and then on to 17,000 tons, a new *King Edward VII.* has been designed, 521½ feet (159 meters) in length, with a beam of 82 feet (25 meters) and mean draught of $^{274}/_5$ (8.5 meters); with the water-line protected with 12-inch plates, and the battery similarly armoured; having two turrets at each end, each armed with a pair of 12-inch guns, and two central side turrets high up (similar to the two with 8-inch guns in the *Vittorio Emanuele III.*), also armed each with two pieces of 12-inch, and four turrets at the four angles of the upper part of the battery, having each one 12-inch gun.

This vessel has no ports whatever in her armor; she carries no secondary armament at all, but only the usual pieces of small caliber for defense against torpedo attack.

The speed to be realized, as proved by the tank trials, is 24 knots.

Jane's All the World's Fighting Ships, 1903

Cuniberti was not the originator of the dreadnought concept, but his article gave the proposition a galvanizing clarity that helped to accelerate the British development program. Cuniberti himself would never actually design a dreadnought (he died in 1913), but some historians regard his article as a form of a literary starting gun for the dreadnought arms race. In so doing, some have even seen Cuniberti as an implicit driving force in the rush to war in 1914.

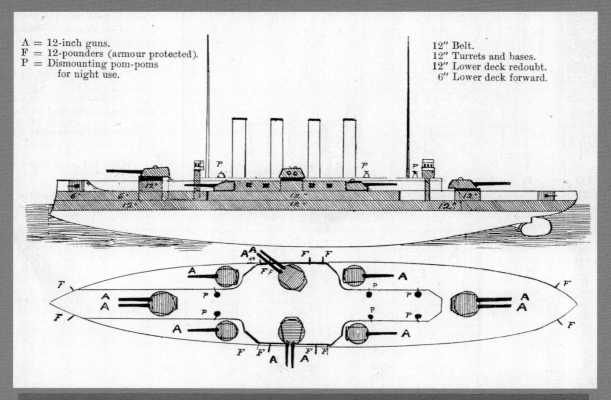

Vittorio Cuniberti's 1903 vision for an "all-big-gun" battleship—in this case 12-inch guns—with heavy armor (represented by the shaded areas) clarified the dreadnought concept.

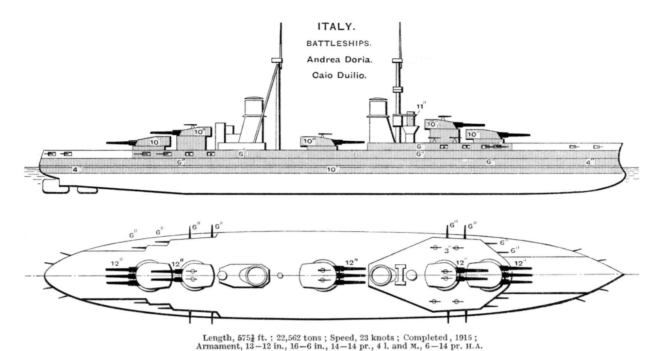

ITALY.

BATTLESHIPS.

Andrea Doria.

Caio Duilio.

Length, 575¼ ft. ; 22,562 tons ; Speed, 23 knots ; Completed , 1915 ;
Armament, 13—12 in., 16—6 in., 14—14 pr., 4 l. and M., 6—14 pr. H.A.

N.B.—In the next succeeding class, Francesco Morosini, Caracciolo, Cristoforo Colombo, and Marcantonio Colonna, eight 15-in. guns were
being mounted in four turrets on the middle line, as in the Queen Elizabeth. Work on these vessels has been stopped.

Right elevation and deck plan diagrams depicting Italian *Andrea Doria*-class battleship, as shown in Brassey's *Naval Annual* of 1915.

From its laying down in June 1909, it took an age for the *Dante Alighieri* to reach commission in 1913. Nor did it have a particularly productive war career. But it began a run of Italian dreadnought shipbuilding, first with the three ships (*Leonardo da Vinci*, *Conte di Cavour*, and *Giulio Cesare*) of the *Conte di Cavour* class (built 1910–15) then the pair of vessels (*Andrea Doria* and *Caio Duilio*) built in 1912–16. There was actually little to separate the two classes. The *Andrea Doria* had a displacement of 24,729 tons, a top speed of 21 knots (24mph) and was positively bristling with armament—13 × 30.5cm (12in) guns in three triple and two twin turret arrangements, plus 35 small-caliber guns for closer-range protection.

Turning to Russia, by the time *Dreadnought* was launched the Tsarist state was reeling from its crushing maritime defeat in the Russo-Japanese War, partly the result of chronic underinvestment in its navy. From 1908, therefore, Russia began pursuing a dreadnought building program, and ultimately produced seven vessels between 1908 and the end of World War I. The *Gangut* class battleships (*Gangut*, *Poltava*, *Petropavlovsk*, and *Sevastopol* were developed specifically for operational use in the Baltic and were 24,400-ton ships with a brisk top speed of 24.1 knots (28mph)—courtesy of four steam turbines and four shafts—and armed with 12 × 30.5cm (12in) guns in four triple turrets. The entire hulls of the ships received armor plate, although this meant that the waterline belt had to be reduced to a maximum thickness of 8.9 inches. The succeeding *Imperatritsa Mariya* class, however, had a slightly thicker armor at the waterline (maximum 10.33 inches). Overall, the ships were smaller (23,413 tons displacement), but they kept the same main armament arrangement as the *Gangut* class. There were three vessels in this class: *Imperatritsa Mariya*, *Imperatritsa Ekaterina Velikaya* (renamed *Svobodnaya Rossiya* in 1917), and *Imperator Aleksander III* (renamed *Volya* in 1917), and all were destined for inauspicious service in the Black Sea.

The *Imperatritsa Mariya*, laid down on October 30, 1911, was the lead ship of its class. Here we see it at anchor on June 24, 1915, with a mooring boom extended from the bows.

The Japanese super-dreadnought *Nagato* at anchor, around September 1924. The ship had a length of 708 feet overall, although the ship was extended further with subsequent modifications. Its long, patchy career ended in the atomic tests at Bikini Atoll in 1946.

The dreadnought USS *Maine* (BB-10) on the Hudson River, New York, December 27, 1918. The most distinctive feature of many U.S. early dreadnoughts was the lattice mast, which were designed for weight saving but were eventually found to be too easily damaged.

between the Royal and Japanese navies at this time was extremely close. They were extremely fast ships, able to hit 27.5 knots (31.6mph) and had big-hitting firepower in the form of 12 × 14in Vickers guns, set in four triple turrets. They were built between 1911 and 1915, overlapping to a large degree with the construction of the *Fuso* class of dreadnoughts—*Fuso* and *Yamashiro*—built between 1912 and 1917 and which would remain in service, with much modernization, until their destruction on the same day, October 25, 1944, at the battle of Leyte Gulf in World War II. They were extremely large vessels at 29,326 tons displacement and had 12 × 14in guns in twin turrets, in a deliberate effort to field warships with greater offensive firepower than the emerging American *New York* class, although by the time they emerged into service there were rival super-dreadnoughts on the world's oceans that could go toe-to-toe with these ships.

Japan produced two more two-ship classes of dreadnoughts by 1921, the *Ise* class of 1915–18 and the *Nagato* class of 1917–21, as the navy worked to fulfil the requirements of its "Eight-Eight Program," an ambition

SMS *Moltke* presents a powerful vision during a visit of a German navy squadron to the United States in 1912. The ship's armor, like that of many German battleships, was the Krupp cemented type, which had both strength and elasticity to resist fracturing and spalling. *Note: Moltke was a battle cruiser*

The U.S. Navy battleship USS *New Mexico* (BB-40) was launched in April 1917. Here we see it in San Pedro, California in 1921.

The entire crew of the USS *Michigan* (BB-27), as photographed on board in Hampton, Virginia, 1918. The total ship's complement was 869 officers and men.

for the navy to have eight first-class battleships and eight battlecruisers. On the other side of the Pacific, however, the United States had by no means been slacking during these years in the development of its own dreadnought and super-dreadnought fleet. Balancing American naval interests between the Atlantic and Pacific Oceans, U.S. naval strategists had been planning a potential Pacific clash with Japan since 1906, and it flexed its muscles in those deep blue waters by sending 16 of its pre-dreadnought battleships on a voyage across the Pacific in 1907.

The first American dreadnought, however, arrived with the USS *South Carolina* (BB-26), launched on July 11, 1908, and commissioned on March 1, 1910. *South Carolina* (BB-26) was the lead ship of a two-ship class—the other vessel was *Michigan* (BB-27). At 16,000 tons, with a top speed of just 18.5 knots (21mph) and with a main armament of 8 × 12in 45-caliber guns, these warships were quickly superseded by other far larger and more potent dreadnoughts running down the slipways. The succeeding *Delaware* class, therefore, were larger (20,380 tons), faster (21 knots/24mph) and better armed, adding another pair Mk V guns. Both ships had different powerplants, *Delaware* (BB-28) with triple-expansion reciprocating engines and *North Dakota* (BB-29) with Curtiss direct-drive steam turbine engines, as a framework for comparison in ultra-long-range Pacific deployments. *North Dakota's* engines proved the least satisfactory, and they were upgraded with more efficient geared turbines by 1917.

These first classes of American dreadnoughts were just the beginning, as the gigantic U.S. industrial capability awakened to produce a long sequence of battleships that reshaped the balance of global naval power. In total, 10 separate classes of dreadnoughts and super-dreadnoughts were built by the United States between

1906 and 1923, the *Delaware* class followed by the *Florida* (2 ships), *Wyoming* (2), *New York* (2), *Nevada* (2), *Pennsylvania* (2), *New Mexico* (3), *Tennessee* (2), and *Colorado* (4 planned, 3 completed) classes. Each class brought its own advances over its predecessors, as some of the most powerful warships on earth came out of American dockyards. The two vessels of the *New York* class—the *New York* (BB-34) and *Texas* (BB-35)—took the firepower up to 10 × 14in guns arranged in five triple turrets, while the subsequent *Nevada* class introduced three-gun turrets (they had two twin and two triple 14-inch turrets) and oil-fired water-tube boilers to the U.S. fleet, plus heavy armor that reached 13.5 inches deep over the magazine and the engineering spaces. Here was an expression of the "all-or-nothing" armor philosophy, in which the most vulnerable or important parts of the ship were very heavily clad in armor, while other less vital spaces received almost nothing, to reduce ship weight. The *New Mexico* and *Tennessee* classes had 12 × 14in guns in four triple turrets, while the *Colorado* class—now 32,600 tons in displacement—had eight 16-inch guns in four twin turrets, these monsters being capable for hurling 2,110lb armor-piercing shells to ranges of more than 19 miles. These programs were the beginning of four decades of naval development that would ultimately make the U.S. Navy the supreme naval power on the planet, as would become evident in World War II, a conflict in which many of the dreadnoughts and super-dreadnoughts, heavily modernized, would serve.

The battleships USS *Nevada* (BB-36) and USS *Oklahoma* (BB-37), both of the *Nevada* class, cut through Atlantic waves during the 1920s. The *Nevada* class represented a revolutionary jump forward in dreadnought design with features such as three-gun turrets, oil-fired water-tube boilers, and "all-or-nothing" armor.

In Profile:
USS *Texas* (BB-35)

The USS *Texas* was a *New York* class battleship, laid down on April 17, 1911, launched on May 18, 1812, and commissioned on March 12, 1914. One of the historically salient points about *Texas* is that it is still with us— *Texas* is today the only surviving dreadnought battleship, displayed and preserved as a museum ship at the San Jacinto Battleground State Historic Park near Houston, Texas. In its long and prestigious history, *Texas* served fully in both world wars. In World War I, *Texas* fired the first American shots of the conflict, when her guns engaged a German U-boat threatening the merchant vessel *Mongolia*, which *Texas* was escorting off the northeast U.S. coast on April 19, 1917. In January 1918 *Texas* crossed the Atlantic and joined the 6th Battle Squadron of Britain's Grand Fleet, assisting the British in performing blockade, patrol, and escort duties.

Although World War I ended in 1918, *Texas* was in for the long haul. Its length of service was only made possible by frequent and significant upgrades, with a major refit in 1925/6, another in 1942, plus numerous other modifications in the 1930s and 1940s that kept the ship safe from obsolescence, including the replacement of coal-fired boilers with oil-fired versions and the installation of extensive anti-aircraft weaponry. As built,

The view forward from behind *Texas*'s centrally positioned funnel. The structure on the top of the boat crane to the left once housed a 3-inch/50-caliber anti-aircraft gun. (Adam Cuerden)

A fine view of the starboard side of USS *Texas*, showing the 5-inch gun aircastles set on the side hull, plus some of the numerous automatic anti-aircraft guns the ship acquired in 1942 and 1944. (Daniel Schwen)

the warship had a displacement of 27,000 long tons and was armed with 10 × 14in guns, 21 × 5in guns, and 10 smaller-caliber weapons. Her maximum speed was 21 knots and range 7,060 miles. By 1945, the ship was displacing 32,000 long tons and in addition to her unchanged 14-inch guns had just six 5-inch guns, but 10 × 3in, 10 x quad 40mm, and 44 × 20mm guns. Her fire control had also been massively upgraded, to include radar systems. While *Texas* eventually looked quite different from the ship that was launched in 1912, the fundamental soundness of its design was nevertheless critical to its longevity.

USS *Texas* in March 1914. The lattice masts were replaced with a tripod version during the ship's modernization overhaul in 1925/6.

USS *Texas* in New York City in 1916. This view shows how virtually the entire after section of the ship was given over to gunnery.

Texas gave solid service in World War II, performing convoy escort but also using her 14-inch guns in offshore naval gunfire support (NGS) for amphibious invasions. The latter included Operation *Torch* off North Africa in October 1942 and adding an enormous weight of fire against German forces around Omaha Beach on D-Day, June 6, 1944, thereafter, continuing to support the advancing U.S. troops in Normandy until June 15. *Texas* subsequently performed the NGS role against the German-occupied port of Cherbourg in late June 1944 and for the Operation *Dragoon* landings in southern France on August 15, before crossing to the other side of the world to add its gunfire to the invasions of both Iwo Jima and Okinawa in 1945, providing both preparatory and on-call bombardments.

Texas was finally decommissioned in 1948, 37 years after it had been laid down, and was immediately designated as a memorial ship in the Port of Houston, the first battleship declared to be a U.S. National Historic Landmark.

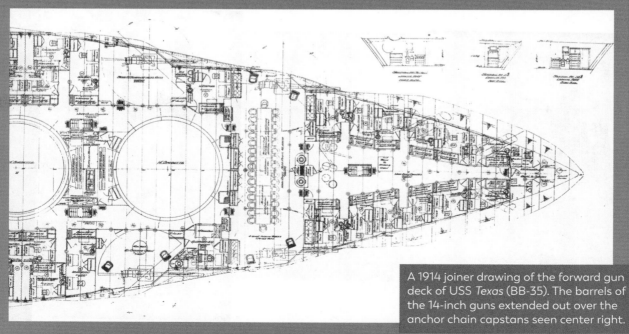

A 1914 joiner drawing of the forward gun deck of USS *Texas* (BB-35). The barrels of the 14-inch guns extended out over the anchor chain capstans seen center right.

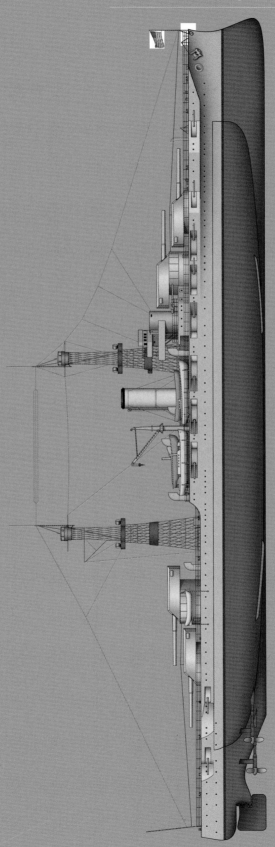

In Profile: *Arizona*

South American Dreadnoughts

While the historical focus of the dreadnought era naturally gravitates towards Europe, South America was also the scene of another dreadnought arms race. This race was principally conducted by the continent's major economic and political rivals, Argentina, Brazil, and Chile, all of which had strong navies and, for a time at least,

The Brazilian dreadnought *Minas Geraes*, here seen in 1942 following a massive reconstruction and modernization at the Rio de Janeiro Naval Yard, including the replacement of its entire boiler system and the rationalization of its funnels from two to one.

The lead ship of the Argentine *Rivadavia* class seen here under construction at the Fore River Shipyard in Quincy, Massachusetts, in 1910. The casemates visible here had armor more than 9 inches thick.

A 1917 artistic impression of Admiral Sir John Jellicoe's flagship *Iron Duke* at anchor with its guns trained to starboard, likely at Scapa Flow.

175

Having opened with the salutary warning of *Audacious,* for now we return to more confident times. Here it would be impossible to look at the operational life of all dreadnoughts and super-dreadnoughts in detail. Instead, we will explore the life of *Dreadnought* herself in the prewar period, then expand this analysis to examine the experience of the battleships during World War I and especially at the battle of Jutland, the defining event of the dreadnought era.

Dreadnought was commissioned to full complement in December 1906. With the dawn of a new year, the first major voyage of her career was the aforementioned Experimental Cruise. This began on January 5, 1907, at Portsmouth and ended on March 23 in the same location, the great ship having journeyed to Spain, Gibraltar, Sardinia, Gibraltar again then across the Atlantic to Trinidad.

Prior to her heading out on this first voyage, it is worth noting that there was some Admiralty concern that the world's docks were not suited to handling such a sizable vessel. On October 9, 1906, an official request went out to the Royal Navy Hydrographer, stating: "The First Sea Lord would be glad if you would kindly let him have, as soon as possible, a list of the Docks, British and Foreign, that at present exist, capable of taking vessels of the 'Dreadnought' size." The reply came back:

> Germany has one dock at Bremerhaven, one at Wilhelmshaven and 2 completing at the latter place that should be capable of taking a "Dreadnought."

> France As far as our information goes there are no docks for "Dreadnought" type. Toulon may have one, but we have not sufficient complete dimensions to say positively; there is one building at Brest.

> Italy Naples has a dock building that may possibly take a "Dreadnought."

> Japan has one at Nagasaki.

> America has one at San Francisco, and 3 building (Norfolk, Philadelphia, Brooklyn).

> England One at Hebburn on Tyne. One at Southampton. One at Birkenhead (2 building). Possibly one at Liverpool and at Glasgow. One building at Belfast.

From this list it is understandable that *Dreadnought* was creating a new world of logistical issues, but those do not seem to have given much cause for concern during her Experimental Cruise. A week's taste of the daily report on the Experimental Cruise provides not just a sense of the ship finding its feet, but also of the general experience of daily life aboard a peacetime dreadnought during this era:

Date	Drills, &c, carried out
Saturday, 5th January 1907. Spithead and at sea.	Sailed from Portsmouth, 8 a.m.
Monday, 7th January 1907. At sea and Arosa Bay.	3.40 p.m.—Arrived and anchored in Arosa Bay. Lieutenant Dreyer joined ship from 'Exmouth.'
Tuesday, 8th January 1907. Arosa Bay and at sea.	A.m. Exercised "out port T.O. net defense" (1st time). Prepared ship for sea. P.m., 3.45—Weighed and proceeded for Gibraltar.
Wednesday, 9th January 1907.	Hands employed in mustering bags. Preparing 12-pr. loader and deflection teachers. Clearing up magazines and shell rooms, &c.

Thursday, 10th January 1907. Gibraltar.	6.5 [*sic*]—Carried out turning trials. 9.0 a.m.—secured to Nos. 9 and 10 buoys, Gibraltar. Prepared ship for coaling. P.m.—Coal lighters came alongside.
Friday, 11th January 1907.	Coaled ship, 1,780 tons.
Saturday, 12th January 1907. Gibraltar.	Cleaned ship throughout after coaling. Took in oil from S.S. "Petroleum."
Monday, 14th January 1907. Gibraltar and at sea.	Prepared ship for sea. 11.10—Slipped and proceeded for Aranci Bay. Y turret's crew and seven 12-prs. crews under instruction. Night—All searchlights, crew, and control parties exercised, burning searchlights.

The Experimental Cruise, and various other maneuvers and trials in her first year of service, proved *Dreadnought* as a seaworthy vessel of good handling. A document entitled "Secret, H.M.S. 'Dreadnought' (Notes for use of the Parliamentary Secretary in Debate)" from this time gives several reassuring defenses of the warship against her potential detractors:

> The official turning trials showed that the "Dreadnought" is, for a ship of her length, remarkable handy. Comparing her performances on trial and those of recently designed battleships, it is found that where the speeds are equal (12 knots) she turns on approximately the same circle as ships of the "King Edward VII" class and on a smaller circle than earlier battleships of the "Duncan," "Formidable," and "Canopus" classes, although the latter are from 90 to 100 feet shorter than the "Dreadnought."
>
> At a speed of 19 knots the "Dreadnought's" tactical diameter is only 25 yards in excess of that of the "King Edward VII" at 16 knots, and is smaller than that of the "Duncan," "Formidable," and "Canopus" classes at speeds of from 15½ to 16½ knots.
>
> But her handiness in open water, due to the smaller tactical diameter at all speeds, is not the only point in her favor. She showed none of that tendency to yaw and to be wild on her helm which is to be noticed not only in battleships but in the longer armored cruisers; when swinging under helm, she was easily steadied by righting the helm when ¾ of a point off the course and meeting her with a few degrees of the opposite helm; it is the custom of all large ships to ease the helm from 1¼ to 1½ points off the course, and it is often necessary to employ as much as 15' of opposite helm to stop the swing and steady the ship.
>
> When turning from rest under the screws she was also very handy and readily turned either up to or off the wind and sea, which is by no means a characteristic of the battleships and large cruisers built since 1890 and which have inward turning screws.

The report paints a favorable picture of the vessel's performance, although given the purpose of the document the reviewer is obviously loading his observation towards the lighter side. As we have seen at several points already in this book, the Experimental Cruise also highlighted a long list of issues that needed to be remedied.

From 1908 until 1914, *Dreadnought* passed her time in the same fashion as most other capital ships of this era. The naval year was usually spent conducting trials, maneuvers, and gunnery training; participating in reviews and strategic exercises with the wider fleet; and spending time in dock for repairs and refits. In terms of the ship's foreign adventures, in 1908 and 1909 she conducted strategic exercises and maneuvers in the Atlantic with elements of the Home and Atlantic Fleets, and similar exercises with the Home, Atlantic, and Mediterranean Fleets off the northwest coast of Spain in early 1911 and 1912. (Another landmark of 1912

This colorized photograph show the *Derfflinger*-class battlecruiser SMS *Hindenburg* at anchor following the internment of the High Seas Fleet at Scapa Flow in 1918.

179

An artistic impression of the sinking of the armored cruisers *Aboukir*, *Hogue*, and *Cressy* by submarine attack on September 22, 1914.

was serving as a target tug in Bantry Bay for HMS *Thunderer* and *Orion*; *Thunderer* was in the process of testing out a new director system.) On September 22, 1913, *Dreadnought* sailed for the Mediterranean, where she remained for the rest of the year, conducting exercises with the 1st and 4th Battle Squadrons and the 3rd Cruiser Squadron, among other events, before heading back to Britain in April 1914. Just three months later, *Dreadnought* and the rest of the Royal Navy's fleets would be at war.

Dreadnoughts at War, 1914–18

If we maintain a strict focus on dreadnoughts and super-dreadnoughts, the ship-vs-ship combat experience gained by these vessels from the outset of the war until the battle of Jutland in late May 1916 was fairly minimal. The reasons behind this were partly matters of grand strategy, but also reflected in incipient concerns about the vulnerability of great warships. In terms of the strategy on the British side, the main role of the Grand Fleet was to implement a maritime blockade of Germany, cutting off the Second Reich's overseas supplies by enforcing naval barriers between Orkney and Norway and also across the Straits of Dover. The blockade would be something that the Royal Navy ultimately did with considerable success, and the maritime chokehold

The Royal Navy battlecruiser HMS *Inflexible* picks up survivors from the German cruiser SMS *Gneisenau* after the battle of the Falkland Islands, December 1914.

would be a key factor in Germany's eventual defeat in 1918. Yet this was essentially a heavy-handed policing role, primarily in deep and open northern waters. The ability of the Royal Navy to venture closer to enemy-controlled coastlines and Kaiserliche Marine naval bases was extremely limited owing to extensive fields of sea mines laid by the Germans off Heligoland and the Frisian coasts, plus the growing threat of submarines and fast torpedo attacks from destroyers. Germany was by and large content at first to take a defensive posture. Over time, it looked to increasingly to its U-boat fleet to take the war to the enemy, while also attempting to create a moment of opportunity to split the Royal Navy's forces and inflict a compelling surface victory.

This is not to say that the early months of the war were free from naval drama and incident. There were clashes between capital ships, with lessons learned. At the battle of Heligoland Bight on August 28, 1914, the German Navy lost three light cruisers and a torpedo boat after German forces were drawn into an ambush by a mixed British force that included five battlecruisers. The score card was horribly balanced out on September

The German armored cruiser SMS *Blücher* begins to capsize after receiving multiple hits from British warships at the battle of Dogger Bank, 25 January 1915.

20, 1914, in an astonishing incident, when the U-boat *U-9* sank three obsolete Royal Navy cruisers—*Aboukir*, *Cressy*, and *Hogue*—of the 7th Cruiser Squadron in the Broad Fourteens, North Sea, with the loss of some 1,450 British lives. The disparity between the attacking vessel and those sunk was a compelling augur of future realities. The surface action off Coronel, Chile, on November 1, 1914, saw the British lose two armored cruisers (*Good Hope* and *Monmouth*) to the more capable *Scharnhorst* and *Gneisenau*, but in turn both of these vessels were sunk, as well as two German light cruisers, at the subsequent battle of the Falkland Islands on December 8, the large British retributory force including the battlecruisers *Invincible* and *Inflexible*.

Actually an armored cruiser; see P. 38-39

At the battle of Dogger Bank on January 24, 1915, the German battlecruisers *Seydlitz*, *Moltke*, *Derfflinger*, and *Blücher* came to blows with Admiral David Beatty's Battlecruiser Force, consisting of *Lion*, *Tiger*, *Princess Royal*, *New Zealand*, and *Indomitable*. (The order of battle also included a heavy cruiser presence on both sides, plus 18 torpedo boats on the German side, with the British being overall numerically superior.) The exchanges of fire began at 20,000 yards, illustrating that the justifications for the big-gun armament were definitely warranted. Both sides took some serious hits, but the German force came off the worse for the encounter, with *Blücher* sunk and *Seydlitz* severely damaged, although there were recriminations that Beatty's force had let the other enemy warships escape.

These early naval battles of World War I provided some food for thought for both navies. One of the dispiriting observations was the poor accuracy of naval gunnery, a lesson that would return again in force at Jutland. For example, the Royal Navy had managed to pull off a victory at the Falkland Islands, but it had fired 1,174 rounds of 12-inch shells alone to pull it off. The *U-9* incident was also one of a widening range of encounters with submarine threats. On August 8, 1914, the *Orion*-class super-dreadnought HMS *Monarch* dodged torpedoes fired at it from *U-15* near Fair Isle, the first such attack on a British battleship in the war. *Dreadnought* came even closer to a German U-boat on March 18, 1915. On that day *Dreadnought* was sailing

HMS *Dreadnought* Captains (including known dates of appointment)

- Captain Reginald H. S. Bacon July 2, 1906–
- Captain Charles E. Madden   August 12, 1907–December 1, 1908
- Captain Charles Bartolomé   December 1, 1908–February 24, 1909
- Captain A. Gordon H. W. Moore   December 1, 1908–July 30, 1909
- Captain Herbert W. Richmond   July 30, 1909–April 4, 1911
- Captain Sydney R. Fremantle   March 28, 1911–December 17, 1912
- Captain Wilmot S. Nicholson   December 17, 1912–July 1, 1914
- Captain William J. S. Alderson   July 1, 1914–July 19, 1916
- Captain John W. L. McClintock   July 19, 1916–December 1, 1916
- Captain Arthur C. S. H. D'Aeth   December 1, 1916–
- Captain Thomas E. Wardle   January 1918–April 20, 1918
- Captain Maurice S. FitzMaurice   April 20 1918–October 5,1918
- Captain Robert H. Coppinger   February 25, 1919–31 March 31, 1920

home with the 4th Battle Squadron following exercises off Pentland Firth, when suddenly *U-29*, captained by Kapitänleutnant Otto Weddigen, broke surface ahead. The submarine had actually just fired a torpedo at HMS *Neptune* (the torpedo missed) and now found itself in the path of *Dreadnought*, which had set course to ram. The battleship squarely connected with the diminutive submarine, cutting *U-29* in half and sinking it with the loss of all hands. Apart from this action, however, *Dreadnought* was not really involved in the shooting war, and was undergoing a refit at the time of the battle of Jutland. However, the Royal Navy's U-boat encounters were but a shadow of the threat the submarines posed to merchant shipping, and in 1915 Germany opted for the first of several periods of unrestricted submarine warfare against merchant vessels, a campaign that the hulking dreadnoughts and battlecruisers could do little to counter until sensible convoy and escort tactics were adopted late in the war.

Generally, though, battles between the opposing capital ships were infrequent in the first two years of the war, and while battlecruisers were engaged, the big dreadnoughts and super-dreadnoughts had yet to prove their investment. That was all to change at Jutland.

The Battle of Jutland

The prelude to the battle of Jutland, the greatest clash of big-gun capital warships in history, can be traced back to November 3, 1914, when German destroyers shelled Great Yarmouth, and December 16, when far larger German naval forces, including five battlecruisers, pounded Scarborough, Whitby, and Hartlepool. Although the actual destruction caused was limited and local, the primary intentions behind the raids were to split the Royal Navy's basing of its warships (which it achieved, the capital warships being divided between Rosyth and Cromarty) and to bring out piecemeal British warship units into open battle—the battle of Dogger Bank was one result.

Jump forward to the spring of 1916, and the German Navy was now looking to elicit a more decisive surface action. On May 31, 1916, the German Hochseeflotte (High Seas Fleet) under Admiral Reinhard Scheer, plus heavy scouting forces commanded by Admiral Franz von Hipper, sailed out into the North Sea, intent on forcing a decisive combat with elements of the British Grand Fleet, particularly Vice-Admiral David Beatty's 1st Battlecruiser Squadron. The German scouting force alone comprised five battlecruisers and 35 other vessels, while the main element totalled 22 dreadnoughts, super-dreadnoughts or battlecruisers, as well as 37 other warships. The plan was to entice the British to commit themselves to a North Sea battle, where they would be hit hard by U-boat attacks and long-range gunnery. *No battlecruisers in German main element*

Yet ironically, Admiral John Jellicoe, the commander of the Grand Fleet, was also planning a major naval operation at this time, involving a major portion of his command. Thus, once radio intercepts on May 30 indicated that the High Seas Fleet was on the move and heading for open waters, the entire British Grand Fleet and Beatty's Battlecruiser Force were quickly mobilized and set sail to intercept. Twenty-four of the 99 ships in this force were dreadnoughts, plus there were 52 ships in Beatty's battlecruiser formation, with six battlecruisers and four super-dreadnoughts forming its big-gun element. The scene was set for the most bruising of naval encounters.

For some hours, the two sides moved in a complex dance as they attempted to find and intercept one another, the precise composition of the opposing forces being unclear to each side. Beatty's force was separate from Jellicoe's, with the battlecruisers farther to the south, heading towards the northern Danish coast, while the Grand Fleet was to the north and west, the two elements hoping to achieve a vast pincer movement around

Vice-Admiral Hipper (center), commander of the of the I Scouting Group at the battle of Jutland, stands with fellow senior Kaiserliche Marine officers in 1916.

the German force. Meanwhile, von Hipper's I Scouting Group, followed by Scheer leading the entire High Seas Fleet, was steaming up from the south, approaching the entrance to the Skagerrak, having left the safety of the mined coastal areas.

On the afternoon of May 31, the chance sighting by both sides of the Danish steamer *N.J. Fjord* led Beatty's and Hipper's vanguards to identify one another and at 1548 hours the battle commenced, with heavy fire at 16,500-yard range. The opening stages of the battle, known as the "Run to the South," did not go to plan for Beatty, even though he initially had a numerical advantage, with six battlecruisers compared to the German's five. *Lion* and *Princess Royal* took on *Seydlitz*, while each of the other British battlecruisers technically fired on one German ship apiece, although a signaling mistake meant that *Tiger* and *New Zealand* both engaged *Moltke*. Hipper's battlecruisers quickly began scoring hits in demonstrations of superior gunnery. *Tiger* was struck nine times in quick succession. *Lion*—Beatty's flagship—had its "Q" turret wiped out by a 30.5cm (12in) shell from *Lützow*. Then, at 1602 hours, the battlecruiser *Indefatigable* was obliterated by three 28cm (11in) shells from *Von der Tann*, the British ship torn apart in two immense magazine explosions that killed all but two of its 1,019 crew. Horrifyingly, *Derfflinger* performed a similar feat on the battlecruiser *Queen Mary*, killing another 1,266 men, although before her destruction *Queen Mary* had inflicted several very heavy hits on *Seydlitz*. Beatty pressed his attack, but then found himself facing the entire High Seas Fleet coming up from the south. This

"Aerial view of the battle of Jutland" by William Lionel Wyllie, the artwork giving an impression of the vast spaces over which the battle was fought.

The battleships *Revenge* (left) and *Hercules* (right) seen en route to the battle of Jutland on May 31, 1916.

Vice-Admiral Sir David Beatty commanded the 1st Battlecruiser Squadron at the battle of Jutland. After the destruction of two of his battlecruisers, he remarked: "There seems to be something wrong with our bloody ships today."

forced him to flee in a running battle—the "Run to the North"—that lasted two hours and saw strikes on both sides, but now Beatty was drawing Scheer and Hipper directly into the path of Jellicoe's Grand Fleet.

Around 1800 hours, Jellicoe had first sighting of Beatty's warships coming up from the south, but communications issues meant that he had little information to go on regarding the precise movements and positing of the High Seas Fleet. When Beatty finally gave him the piece of crucial information, Jellicoe ordered his battleships into a classic single battle line, crossing Scheer's "T" and presenting the greatest number of broadside barrels to face the enemy.

The epic clash, in effect the moment that the dreadnought arms race had been leading to, came much to Scheer's shock at 1830 hours, when Jellicoe's Grand Fleet began firing its first shells at the German ranks. Awe-inspiring firepower was unleashed, in which both fleets took hits and fatalities. The armored cruiser HMS *Defence* was annihilated in a magazine explosion after multiple strikes, and *Warrior* and *Warspite* were also severely damaged. *Indomitable* scored hits on *Derfflinger* and *Seydlitz*, while *Lutzow* was struck 10 times by shells from *Lion*, *Inflexible*, and *Invincible*. Then *Lützow* and *Derfflinger* landed salvoes on *Invincible*, again causing a magazine explosion that ripped the ship apart and sank it in 90 seconds—only six of the ship's 1,032 officers and men survived.

Although the High Seas Fleet was holding its own, Scheer recognized that he was outnumbered, outgunned, and outmaneuvered by the British. Taking the advantage of fading light, Scheer now began the process of disengaging and fleeing southeast to safety, although he took his forces briefly back into action around 7 p.m., attempting to take advantage of a perceived (but incorrect) split in the British fleet, before again turning towards safety. Fighting rumbled on sporadically into the early hours of June 1. Key events of the night action were the sinking of the pre-dreadnought SMS *Pommern* by British destroyer torpedo attacks, the destruction of the *Duke of Edinburgh*-class armored cruiser *Black Prince* by *Thüringen* and other warships, and the final scuttling of the

HMS *Queen Mary* is blown to pieces at the battle of Jutland. To the left is the battlecruiser HMS *Lion*, surrounded by waterspouts from enemy shots falling short.

The battlecruiser HMS *Tiger* was hit 14 times during the battle of Jutland. Here we see the crushing damage inflicted on one of her barbettes. Ten of her crew members were killed during the action.

The battlecruiser HMS *Invincible* explodes in a ball of flame, May 31, 1916; 1,026 officers and men were killed.

Shell damage inflicted on the forward superstructure of *Colossus* at the battle of Jutland in 1916. Remarkably, there were no fatalities, and only six men were injured.

crippled battlecruiser *Lützow*. But eventually, the two sides broke apart entirely and headed back to their bases to count the cost.

A political and public controversy raged after the battle, as both sides declared victory. When the final accounting was taken, the British had lost three battlecruisers, three armored cruisers, and eight destroyers, plus 5,069 dead mariners. On the German side, the final tally was one battleship, one battlecruiser, three cruisers, and five destroyers, with 2,115 dead. The Germans could certainly claim a material victory, but at the strategic level the battle demonstrated how the High Seas Fleet was incapable, ultimately, of breaking the Royal Navy and the blockade it had imposed upon the Fatherland.

With full recognition of the human cost of the battle, Jutland was nevertheless an epic laboratory for educating the British about the combat readiness of its navy. Several key lessons emerged, painfully, from the action. There was the need for more effective scouting and reconnaissance procedures, and also for improvements in inter-ship wireless communications. There was a paramount need to improve gunnery, as it was felt that the Germans demonstrated a greater skill in fire control. The effect of British hits on German vessels was limited by the fact that British shells broke up more quickly on first impact than German shells; if the British shells had had more convincing penetration, Jutland might have been an undeniable British victory. The destruction of the three battlecruisers highlighted the most lessons—the need for British warships to have adequate armor arrangements and, especially, better procedures for handling sensitive cordite charges, to as much as possible prevent the catastrophic magazine detonations seen during the clash. The post-Jutland debates were complex, and remain so today, with a dispute still alive about the rights and wrongs of British warship design. Some of the official recommendations to emerge were collected as follows:

Admiral John Rushworth Jellicoe, who commanded the Grand Fleet at Jutland.

IRON DUKE

H.M.S. "IRON DUKE"

S403-13

HMS *Iron Duke* was a major player in the battle of Jutland in 1916, hitting *König* with a 13.5-inch shell.

A photograph of the forward port side of HMS *Warspite*, showing the penetration and splinter damage caused by a German shell at the battle of Jutland.

10. Points particularly recommended for investigation: (a) The position of magazines—whether they should not all be placed as low as possible in a ship, and on the center line. (b) The protection of magazines from shell fire and torpedoes. Observing that the penetration of one hot splinter to a magazine may be sufficient to cause explosion of the contents. (c) The need of additional protection to roof plates, glacis, trunk of all turrets, and particularly of "Q" turret, since most hits occur on this central part of ships.

(d) The British design of turret, with sloping front and roof plates, increases the chance of penetration by shell at long range by providing a surface nearer the normal than if the front plates were vertical and the roof plates horizontal. (e) The provision of a separate explosion trunk from all handing rooms to the upper deck, to provide some egress for gas pressures other than through the trunk and turret. (f) The design of flash doors throughout 13.5' and 12' turrets appears to have been based only on the necessity of defeating back flame from the gun, which is small in volume and produces no gas pressure comparable with that of a shell burst or ignition of cordite in the turret. The numerous holes in gunhouse and working chamber floors and sides are a decided source of danger.

(g) The abolition of igniters permanently fitted to charges. (h) The protection of charges by a light metal envelope capable of volatilization on firing. (i) The apparent immunity of German nitro-cellulose propellants from explosion by shell fire, as compared with cordite. (j) The ready communication of explosion from one magazine to another widely separated. (k) The safety of nose-fuzes in common H.E. shell. (l) The stowage of shell in bins in gunhouses and working chambers of turrets. (m) The introduction of the Q.F. principle of Breech Mechanism for all future guns.

David Beatty, letter to the Permanent Secretary to the Board of Admiralty,
Sir W. Graham Greene, July 14, 1916

All of these factors fed, to a greater or lesser extent, into post-war battleship design. Yet in some ways, even Jutland demonstrated that the era of the dreadnought and super-dreadnought was already waning. There would always be a limit to how heavily a warship could be armored before it became unwieldy. However, there was also the recognition that the vertical armor configuration of the big battleships had to change to give more deck protection from plunging long-range fire. It was this process of redesign, plus a gradual increase in the volume of secondary armament, that fed into the post-World War I era of the battleship, and the notion of the all-big-gun dreadnought and super-dreadnought began to slip from use. After Jutland, the fleets never went head-to-head again, each side realizing that the risk was too great. World War I therefore ended with many authorities openly questioning the relevance of battleships as influential weapons of war.

SMS *Seydlitz* to port after the battle of Jutland, having taken 5,300 metric tons of water following shell and torpedo strikes.

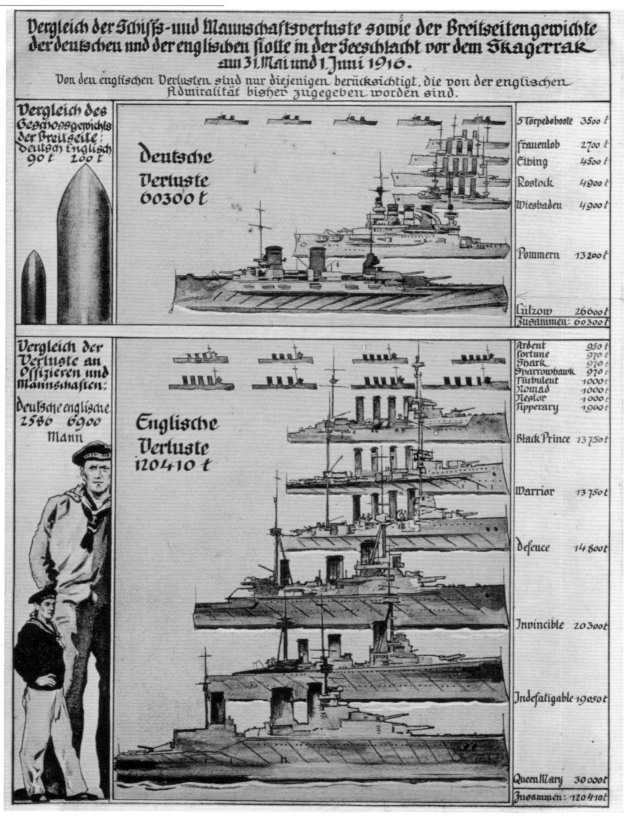

Vergleich der Schiffs- und Mannschaftsverluste sowie der Breitseitengewichte der deutschen und der englischen Flotte in der Seeschlacht vor dem Skagerrak am 31. Mai und 1. Juni 1916.

Von den englischen Verlusten sind nur diejenigen berücksichtigt, die von der englischen Admiralität bisher zugegeben worden sind.

Vergleich des Geschossgewichts der Breitseite: deutsch englisch 90 t 200 t

deutsche Verluste 60300 t

5 Torpedoboote	3500 t
Frauenlob	2700 t
Elbing	4500 t
Rostock	4900 t
Wiesbaden	4900 t
Pommern	13200 t
Lützow	26600 t
Zusammen:	60300 t

Vergleich der Verluste an Offizieren und Mannschaften: deutsche englische 2536 6900 Mann

Englische Verluste 120410 t

Ardent	950 t
Fortune	970 t
Shark	970 t
Sparrowhawk	970 t
Turbulent	1000 t
Nomad	1000 t
Nestor	1000 t
Tipperary	1900 t
Black Prince	13750 t
Warrior	13750 t
Defence	14800 t
Invincible	20300 t
Indefatigable	19050 t
Queen Mary	30000 t
Zusammen:	120410 t

[handwritten margin note: The German made an error on one of their own ships, using a drawing of Seydlitz in place of Lützow]

A German poster from June 1917 explains the rationale behind declaring the battle of Jutland a German victory.

In Profile:
Witness to Jutland

The guns were loaded and brought to the half cock and reported, and then came the order to bring the right gun to the ready … Shortly after this, the first salvo was fired, and we started on the great game.

Up till now I had not noticed any noise, such as being struck by a shell, but afterwards there was a heavy blow, struck, I should imagine, in the after 4-inch battery, and a lot of dust and pieces flying around on the top of "X" turret.

The British battlecruiser HMS *Indefatigable* sinks after being struck by shells from the German battlecruiser *Von der Tann* at Jutland, the resulting magazine explosion destroying the ship.

Another shock was felt shortly after this, but it did not affect the turret, so no notice was taken. Then the T.S. reported to Lt Ewert that the third ship of the line was dropping out. First blood to Queen Mary.

A few more rounds were fired when I took another look through my telescope and there was quite a fair distance between the second ship and what I believed was the fourth ship, due I think to third ship going under. Flames were belching from what I took to be the fourth ship of the line, then came the big explosion which shook us a bit, and on looking at the pressure gauge I saw the pressure had failed. Immediately after that came, what I term, the big smash, and I was dangling in the air on a bowline, which saved me from being thrown down on the floor of the turret.

Petty Officer Ernest Francis, gunner's mate, *Queen Mary*

The destructive force of naval gunnery is evident in this photograph of the German battlecruiser SMS *Seydlitz* in harbor after the battle of Jutland.

The Imperial Japanese Navy battleship *Yamashiro* undergoes initial trials off Tateyama, Japan, in December 1916.

In Profile:
HMS *Caroline*—The Last Survivor of Jutland

Today there is one survivor from the battle of Jutland itself. Although not a dreadnought or super-dreadnought vessel, it nevertheless provides a unique window into the Royal Navy of World War I. HMS *Caroline*, a C-class light cruiser, was laid down in 1914 but in one form or another survived as functioning MOD [Ministry of Defense] property until 2011. Since then, it has been deservedly saved from demolition, and has undergone a painstaking restoration to bring it to life for the general public, as a museum ship in the Alexandra Graving Dock in Belfast.

Caroline was the lead ship of a six-ship class, consisting of *Caroline, Carysfort, Cleopatra, Comus, Conquest,* and *Cordelia*. (Note, however, that sometimes this class is referred to as the *Comus* class.) It was ordered within the 1913 program and was to be constructed by the Cammell Laird shipbuilder at Birkenhead. The ship was laid down on January 28, 1914, and launched almost exactly eight months later, on September 29. Her overall length was 446 feet, with a beam of 41.5 feet and a maximum draught of 16 feet. Displacement, in loaded state, was

A fine starboard-side view of HMS *Caroline*. Note the distinctive triple-funnel design—all three funnels remain in situ on the restored ship.

Caroline as she stands today at Alexandra Graving Dock in Belfast, just a few hundred yards from where *Titanic* was constructed.

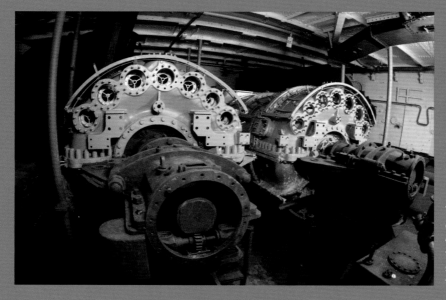

The Parsons turbines on *Caroline* generated 40,000shp and drove four shafts. This image shows the turbines prior to their restoration.

One of the most impressive sections of *Caroline* is the emergency steering gear down in the lower aft hull. If the standard steering gear was knocked out, crew members could manually move the rudder via the bank of wooden ship's wheels, geared directly to the rudder. Directional information was given on an overhead dial, which was moved by a system of geared linkages.

4,219 tons. For propulsion, *Caroline* was powered by four-shaft Parsons turbines generating 40,000shp, giving a maximum speed of 28.5 knots (32mph). Note, however, that to its detriment *Caroline* did not have geared turbines, a fact that reduced its performance at lower speeds. Later ships of the C class did have the geared powerplant.

In terms of armament, as-built *Caroline* had 2 × BL 6in/45 Mk XII guns, both set aft in single mounts, plus 8 × QF 4in/45 Mk V guns (two forward, three on each beam), one 6-pdr gun and 4 × 21in torpedo tubes. The decision to mount both 6-inch guns aft was taken to make fire-control easier, and to give the main armament a better platform in rough seas. *Caroline*'s original armament configuration, and indeed that of many of those in the C class, was changed significantly between 1914 and 1918, based on combat feedback and comparison with German armament set-ups. The 4-inch guns forward were replaced in 1916 by another 6-inch single, and a 4-inch HA gun for anti-aircraft work replaced the 3-pdr. Gradually all 4-inch guns were removed and replaced with 4-inch HA weapons, and a fourth 6-inch gun was mounted on a platform abaft the funnels. Experience showed that the heavier 6-inch guns had a superior tactical performance to the 4-inch weapons, hence the gravitation in that direction.

By the time *Caroline* was commissioned into service on December 4, 1914, World War I was already underway, so the ship went straight into wartime operations. This initially meant conducting patrols in the North Sea and also forming part of convoy screens, protecting vulnerable merchant ships against the depredations of German U-boats and surface vessels. *Caroline* performed these duties without firing a shot in anger. Indeed, its guns might have stayed silent for the entire war had it not been involved in the greatest naval surface engagement in history, the battle of Jutland on May 31–June 1, 1916. An urgent steering gear repair

Caroline's bridge and navigating platform. Reconstruction has revealed the brass framework that insulated the bridge instruments from electromagnetic interference. (Jef Maytom)

meant that *Caroline* didn't leave Scapa Flow to join the Grand Fleet until the evening of May 30, after which she took up position in the fleet screening force, one of a number of ships trying to spot the German High Seas Fleet, while acting as a protective shield to the major warships. At around 1807 hours on May 31, *Caroline* was drawn into the growing shooting battle, witnessing the battlecruiser *Invincible* blowing up. Then at 1930 hours *Caroline* added its firepower to the clash: at a range of 9,200 yards, *Caroline* fired three 6-inch and four 9-inch rounds at a German destroyer, before disengaging. Then, at 2100 hours, *Caroline* and the light cruiser *Royalist* came into contact with the main German battleline, including the dreadnought *Nassau*. After getting

A steering column connection. One runs down each side of the ship. (Jef Maytom)

clearance to fire from commander of the 2nd Battle Squadron, Admiral Sir Martyn Jerram, both ships launched torpedoes towards the enemy, without result, before retreating under the resultant enemy fire. (One heavy German shell actually passed between the wireless deck and the upper deck.) *Caroline* then returned to Scapa Flow on June 2.

Post-World War I, Caroline was saved from the scrapyard by the formation of the Ulster Division of the Royal Naval Volunteer Reserve (RNVR); *Caroline* was chosen to be the division's drill ship in Belfast. Having been towed to Belfast, the ship needed extensive modification to facilitate her new static role. The adaptation process, performed by Harland & Wolff, included:

- A deckhouse built over the aft upper deck
- Removal of the ship's boilers (the turbines were left in place)
- Conversion of numerous rooms into instruction spaces and workshops.

Eventually anchored in the Musgrave Channel, the modified *Caroline* began its busy life as a training ship.

Caroline dutifully served as a reserve unit until 2009, although during the 1990s there had been some discussion about the Imperial War Museum (IWM) taking it over as an exhibit ship at Hartlepool. In December 2009, however, the ship was decommissioned as a reserve unit and was decommissioned on March 31, 2011. Not wishing to see this historic vessel go to ruin, the National Museum of the Royal Navy (NMRN) took over its care, although the long-term future remained uncertain.

The restoration of HMS *Caroline* is story of vision and determination, plus the successful negotiation of the acres of paperwork that need completing for a viable restoration project. In 2011/12 various proposals about *Caroline* were in discussion, including restoring the entire ship back to a facsimile of its original configuration, and also moving the ship to Portsmouth. In October 2012, however, the Northern Ireland government announced that *Caroline* would stay in Belfast, integrated as it was into the Belfast community, and over the next two years the Heritage Lottery Fund provided the primary means—funding of £12 million—to convert the vessel into a museum ship for the general public. Today that ship gives the public an authentic experience of a Jutland-era warship both above and below decks, and photographs from its restoration phase are included here.

This hatch clearly shows how it could be locked down with brass screws, to shut off oxygen to a fire or to prevent flooding.

In Profile:
The Scuttling of the High Seas Fleet at Scapa Flow

The massive, unified scuttling of the German High Seas Fleet at Scapa Flow in 1919 can perhaps be taken as the most emblematic event signaling the end of the age of the dreadnought. With the Allied victory and the Armistice on November 11, 1918, one of the key elements in the peace negotiations was to decide what would be done with the High Seas Fleet, which was still a magisterial force, with more than 70 major combat vessels. The decision was taken that the entire fleet would be interned in Allied ports until a firm decision was taken. In Operation *ZZ*, Admiral Sir David Beatty would lead out 191 Allied vessels, rendezvous with 70 German warships in the North Sea, commanded by Rear Admiral Ludwig von Reuter, and then lead them back to Scapa Flow in the Orkney Islands, once the ships had been inspected for disarmament compliance. This operation, tense but without violence, took place on November 25–27, 1918, with four more vessels joining shortly after, the last being the dreadnought *Baden* in January 1919.

SMS *Seydlitz*, SMS *Moltke*, and the two remaining *Derfflinger*-class ships, *Hindenburg* and *Derfflinger*, sail towards Scapa Flow and internment, on Thursday November 21, 1918.

At Scapa Flow, the 20,000 German sailors aboard the warships were steadily reduced to skeleton crews, there just to maintain the essential seaworthiness of the vessels. Bored by the following months of inactivity and near-starvation rations and angered by the fact that the fleet was still so powerful and yet had been emasculated, the mood amongst these men became angry and mutinous. Furthermore, von Reuter developed plans to scuttle the fleet, to prevent the ignominy of the vessels ultimately falling into Allied hands. Thus, on the morning of June 21, 1919, with the British fleet absent on exercises, von Reuter ordered his men to open the seacocks and any other underwater apertures, and within five hours 52 of the world's most powerful warships sank beyond rescue (22 were beached by the British). The scuttling saw the world's total of dreadnoughts, super-dreadnoughts, battleships, and battlecruisers drop precipitously in just a few hours. Of these types, the ships lost were *Bayern*, *Friedrich der Grosse*, *Grosser Kurfürst*, *Kaiser*, *Kaiserin*, *König*, *König Albert*, *Kronprinz Wilhelm*, *Markgraf*, *Prinzregent Luitpold*, *Derfflinger*, *Hindenburg*, *Moltke*, *Seydltiz*, and *Von der Tann* (*Baden* was beached). Given that so many of these ships had survived Jutland, it is ironic that peacetime accomplished the destruction that battle had not.

Only the upper works of the German battlecruiser SMS *Hindenburg* remain above the water after scuttling at Scapa Flow, June 1919.

The great battlescruiser HMS *Hood*, destroyed in May 1941 at the battle of Denmark Strait by early salvoes from the German battleship *Bismarck*.

HMS *Repulse* at Haifa in 1938. Few could have foreseen the destruction of this great vessel by Japanese air attack in December 1941.

With the benefit of our hindsight, the prophetic quality of this passage is startling. Scott placed aviation and submarines at the vanguard of naval warfare, with even the great surface vessels essentially looking for a place to hide during wartime. We need only look ahead to the shy deployments of the *Tirpitz* in World War II to see the accuracy of this prediction. Scott was also writing at a time when he couldn't see the eventual combat force of naval aviation, a time when U.S. dive-bombers and torpedo bombers would reduce the largest battleship ever made, the Japanese *Yamato*, to nothing more than useless, blistered metal.

The end of World War I, however, was not the end of the international battleship-building program. Indeed, some of the greatest warships of the Royal Navy's history were launched during the 1920s, 1930s, and 1940s, including the battlecruisers *Tiger*, *Repulse*, and *Hood*, the five ships that composed the *King George V* class, and HMS *Vanguard*, the last battleship in history to be launched, in 1946.

[margin handwritten note: Incorrect — all three battlecruisers were launched before 1920. Tiger 1913, Repulse 1916, Hood 1918]

Even as these ships were being developed and launched, however, the great dreadnoughts and super-dreadnoughts were suffering the depredations of obsolescence. The 1920s was a particularly intense time for the scrapping of dreadnought ships. *Dreadnought* herself went to the scrapper's yard in 1921, as did *Bellerophon*, *Superb*, *St Vincent*, and *Hercules*. The following year they were joined by *Collingwood*, *Neptune*, *Agincourt*, *Conqueror*, and *Orion*. The rate of attrition was rapid, and by 1928 all the British dreadnoughts were gone, plus eight of the super-dreadnoughts. Of the remaining super-dreadnoughts, their advanced firepower and steady modifications ensured that some lasted through the interwar years and even served during World War II, but the new age of naval warfare quickly brought losses for the great warships.

On October 14, 1939, the *Revenge*-class super-dreadnought *Royal Oak* was sunk by U-boat attack while supposedly safe at anchor in Scapa Flow, hit by a single torpedo fired by *U-47* and captained by the future U-boat ace Kapitänleutnant Günther Prien. Some 833 men died. But *Royal Oak* was not the last to go. On November 25, 1941, the *Queen Elizabeth*-class super-dreadnought HMS *Barham* was steaming in the Mediterranean north of Sidi Barrani, Egypt, accompanied by *Queen Elizabeth* herself and another battleship of the class, *Valiant*. Together these three mighty ships plus eight destroyers constituted "Force K," hunting Axis supply convoys attempting to make runs between Italy and North Africa. It must have projected a sense of impregnability, a vision of iron muscle on the Mediterranean waters, but that confidence was about to be torn apart.

At 1625 hours, and at just 750 yards distance from *Barham*, Oberleutnant zur See Hans-Diedrich von Tiesenhausen, the commander of U-boat *U-331*, ordered a spread of torpedoes to be fired at the hulking targets in front of him. Three of them slammed into *Barham*, impacting close together and rending open the hull. As tens of thousands of gallons of seawater rushed into the now-stricken vessel, *Barham* began capsizing to port, dozens of men sliding down or clinging onto the hull. This horrifying development was filmed by Pathé cameraman John Turner, aboard HMS *Valiant*, who also caught what happened next. Just as the foremast settled into the water, *Barham* was virtually obliterated in a thunderous magazine explosion, splitting the ship in two and sending it quickly to the bottom. Within minutes, the only evidence of her existence was a dire pall of smoke hanging over the surface of the waters, and 841 men were dead out of a crew of 1,184.

Just over two weeks after *Barham* was destroyed, the Royal Navy suffered further calamity to its fleet when the *King George V*-class battleship HMS *Prince of Wales* and the battlecruiser *Repulse* were both sunk by Japanese air attack off the coast of Malaya on December 10, 1941. This was the first time in history that capital warships had been sunk by airpower. *[handwritten note: Not true. This was the first time battleships were sunk at sea. Previously, aircraft had sunk battleships in harbor — Taranto (1940) and Pearl Harbor.]*

The fates of *Royal Oak*, *Barham*, *Prince of Wales*, and *Repulse* were emblematic of just how much naval warfare had changed in such a short space of time. Other nations were learning the same lessons, especially the Americans and the Japanese, the former from the attack on the Pacific Fleet at Pearl Harbor on December 7,

1941, and the latter as its great battleships were progressively wiped out between 1942 and 1945 by superior U.S. airpower and submarines. Wartime service, furthermore, could not save surviving super-dreadnoughts from subsequent decommissioning and scrapping. Almost all the global super-dreadnoughts were broken up during the second half of the 1940s, the exception being *Canada*, which was returned to Chile in 1920 and defied the scrapyard until 1959. Today, all that remains of the dreadnought era is the battleship USS *Texas*, an important reminder of an age when battleships were ascendant.

Back in 1906, when *Dreadnought* was emerging onto the world scene, battleships were the true kings of the waves, the most herculean warships yet conceived. Over the course of three decades, however, it became apparent that first submarines and then naval aircraft were the new hunters on the oceans, and battleships were almost unmissable large targets. During World War II, that lesson was learned to such an extent that battleships almost entirely disappeared from fleet compositions. That said, while the tactical performance of the dreadnoughts and super-dreadnoughts is open to question, their influence over world politics, and over the lives of the thousands of men who built or crewed them, is undeniable.

The USS *Pennsylvania* (BB-38) drydocked in an Advanced Base Sectional Dock (ABSD) in the Pacific, c. 1944. Many of the U.S. dreadnoughts and super-dreadnoughts would fight in the Pacific in the World War I, mainly to provide naval gunfire support.

The USS *Arizona* sails through New York during a naval review. As mighty a ship as it was, *Arizona* was destroyed by Japanese air attack at Pearl Harbor on December 7, 1941, with the loss of 1,102 lives.

| Further Reading

Official Admiralty and Royal Navy Primary Source Documents

"Fire Control and Secondary Armament (an answer to the complaint that the *Dreadnought* has insufficient secondary armament)" (July 1906)

"HMS *Dreadnought*—Plans of Decks" (1906)

"HMS *Dreadnought* (Notes for Use of the Parliamentary Secretary in Debate" (June 1906)

"Memorandum Explanatory of the Programme of New Construction for 1905–1906, With Details Omitted from the Navy Estimates For 1906–1907" (1906)

"Naval Strength of Principal Maritime Powers showing in detail Dreadnoughts built, building and projected" (1908)

"The Balance of Naval Power" (1906)

"Turning Powers of the Dreadnought" (1906)

Bacon, Captain R. C. *Report on the Experimental Cruise* (1907)

Director of Naval Ordnance, "Considerations of the design of a battleship" (n.d.)

Naval Controller, "Comparison of various Guns for Secondary Armament of Battleships" (n.d.)

Naval Intelligence Division, "HM ships *Dreadnought* and *Invincible*: memorandum" (n.d.)

Slade, Captain E. J. W., "Lecture on Speed in Battleships" (n.d.)

St. Erme Cardew, John, Journal kept by John St. Erme Cardew as Midshipman on: HMS *Dreadnought* September 15, 1909–September 7, 1910

Books

Allen, Richard W., *Air Supply to Boiler Rooms of Modern Ships of War* (London, Charles Griffin & Co., 1921)

Breyer, Siegfried, *Battleships and Battle Cruisers, 1905–1970*, trans. by Alfred Kurti (London, MacDonald & Jane's, 1973)

Brown, David K. *The Grand Fleet: Warship Design and Development 1906–1922* (Barnsley, Seaforth, 1997)

Burr, Lawrence, *British Battlecruisers 1914–18* (Oxford, Osprey, 2006)

Burt, R. A., *British Battleships of World War One* (Barnsley, Seaforth, 2012)

Buxton, Ian & Ian Johnston, *The Battleship Builders: Constructing and Arming British Capital Ships* (Barnsley, Seaforth, 2013)

Chant, Christopher, *Twentieth-Century War Machines – Sea* (London, Chancellor Press, 1999)

Dawson, Captain Lionel, *Flotillas: A Hard-Lying Story* (London, Rich & Cowen Ltd, 1935)

Draminski, Stefan, *The Battleship HMS Dreadnought (Super drawings in 3D)* (Lublin, Kagero, 2013)

Friedman, Norman, *Naval Firepower: Battleship Guns and Gunnery in the Dreadnought Era* (Barnsley, Seaforth, 2008)

Friedman, Norman, *Naval Weapons of World War One: Guns, Torpedoes, Mines and ASW Weapons of all Nations: An Illustrated Directory* (Barnsley, Seaforth, 2011)

Golding, Harry (ed.), *The Wonder Book of Ships* (London, Ward, Lock & Co., n.d.)

Golding, Harry (ed.), *The Wonder Book of the Navy* (London, Ward, Lock & Co. n.d.)

Hodges, Peter, *The Big Gun: Battleship Main Armament 1860–1945* (London, Conway Maritime Press, 1981)

Hough, Richard, *Dreadnought: A History of the Modern Battleship* (London, Endeavour Press, 2015)

Hythe, Viscount (ed.), *The Naval Annual 1913* (Portsmouth, J. Griffin & Co., 1913)

Jane's Fighting Ships of World War I (London, Studio Editions, 1990)

Keegan, John, *Battle at Sea* (London, Pimlico, 1993)

Konstam, Angus, *British Battleships 1914–18 (1): The Early Dreadnoughts* (Oxford, Osprey, 2013)

Konstam, Angus, *British Battleships 1914–18 (2): The Super-dreadnoughts* (Oxford, Osprey, 2013)

Leather, John, *World Warships in Review 1860–1906* (London, Purnell, 1976)

Parkinson, Roger, *Dreadnought – The ship that changed the world* (London, I. B. Taurus, 2015)

Roberts, John, *The Battleship Dreadnought – Anatomy of the Ship* (London, Conway, 2013)

Thomas, Roger D. & Brian Patterson, *Dreadnoughts in Camera* (Stroud, Sutton, 1998)

| Index

[handwritten annotations:] Latorre — See p.172; Cochrane

Other Titles in the Casemate Illustrated Special Series:

U.S. AIRCRAFT CARRIERS 1939–45
by Ingo Baurnfeind
Extensively illustrated, this volume tells the dramatic story of US aircraft carriers in World War II by class, ranging from early pre-war designs to the gigantic fleet carriers.
JUNE 2021 | 9781612009346

BRITISH FIGHTER AIRCRAFT IN WORLD WAR I: DESIGN, CONSTRUCTION AND INNOVATION
by Mark C. Wilkins
Packed with hundreds of photographs, this volume describes how British aircraft manufacturers vied to create the best fighter to counter German technology during World War I.
MAY 2021 | 9781612008813

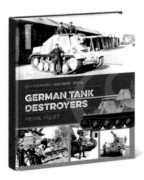

GERMAN TANK DESTROYERS
by Pierre Tiquet
A fully illustrated account of Panzerjägers used by the Wehrmacht during World War II, from the first anti-tank artillery used in 1939, through to the Elefant.
JULY 2021 | 9781612009063

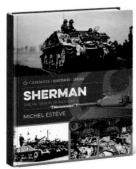

SHERMAN: THE M4 TANK IN WORLD WAR II
by Michel Estève
Fully illustrated, exceptionally detailed account of the development and deployment of the M4 Sherman in World War II.
JULY 2020 | 9781612007397